This book is dedicated to ·

Wiley Mullins, Jr. and Hattie Peoples Mullins, my parents, who unfortunately did not live to enjoy this book, but would have found great pleasure in realizing the impact that they and many of their friends and neighbors had and continue to have on my life's work. They were phenomenal parents to me and my siblings, Michael, Ozzie, and Mary.

Mable Morris Mullins, Julia Gamble Peoples, and Wiley Mullins, Sr., my grandparents, who made growing up close to them a memorable experience every day. Each of them in their own unique way fueled my passion—wellness.

Carol Brooks and Jean Long Graves, two incredible women who through their many acts of kindness to others challenge me to serve mankind with grace, friendship, love, and a smile.

Robert and Edith Keith: A remarkable couple, who as a couple define the word *teamwork*. Together, they tirelessly offer support and care for many people around the world.

Salad Makes the Meal

150 Simple and Inspired Salad Recipes Everyone Will Love

Wiley Mullins
The Salad Man™

RODALE

© 2008 by Wiley Mullins

All rights reserved. No part of this publication may be reproduced or transmitted in any form or by any means, electronic or mechanical, including photocopying, recording, or any other information storage and retrieval system, without the written permission of the publisher.

Rodale books may be purchased for business or promotional use or for special sales. For information, please write to: Special Markets Department, Rodale, Inc., 733 Third Avenue, New York, NY 10017

Printed in the United States of America Rodale Inc. makes every effort to use acid-free ∞, recycled paper ♻.

Illustrations © Rodale Inc.

Book design by Christina Gaugler

Library of Congress Cataloging-in-Publication Data

Mullins, Wiley.

    Salad makes the meal : 150 simple and inspired salad recipes everyone will love / Wiley Mullins.

      p.   cm.

    Includes index.

    ISBN-13 978-1-59486-848-1 paperback

    ISBN-10 1-59486-848-4 paperback

    1. Salads.   I. Title.

TX807.M85 2008

641.8'3—dc22   2007050748

Distributed to the book trade by Macmillan

2 4 6 8 10 9 7 5 3 1 paperback

RODALE
LIVE YOUR WHOLE LIFE™

We inspire and enable people to improve their lives and the world around them For more of our products visit **rodalestore.com** or call 800-848-4735

Contents

Acknowledgments

I'd like to thank the following people for helping to make this book a reality. I am so very appreciative for their thoughts, ideas, and support.

Coleen O'Shea: A terrific agent whose demeanor is quiet, yet strong, continuously offered valuable input to the entire process. Coleen, thanks for taking the time to always listen!

Pamela Cannon: A gifted collaborator, whose unique collection of talents and skills made this effort a wonderful experience and fun, too.

Stephanie Lyness: Her knowledge of good-tasting, good-for-you foods is woven in the recipes throughout this book. Thank you for sharing your wide-ranging knowledge and experience.

Shea Zukowski, Andrew Malkin, and the entire Rodale team: Thank you for everything ranging from your initial support of the concept, to the creation of this book, to the rewarding publishing experience you've afforded me. This has truly been a highlight of my life.

Introduction

Why Salad?

For years, people in the produce business have called me The Salad Man because I'm so passionate about salads.

To me, salads are so amazingly versatile that no meal seems complete without one. Whether it's starting my day with a colorful fruit salad at breakfast, enjoying a sizzling Steak and Tomato Salad with Horseradish Dressing for lunch, or ending my dinner with a sweet and satisfying Banana Pudding Salad, salad is perfect at every meal. I actually consider salads the ultimate comfort food because they are not only soul-satisfyingly delicious, but they are also an important part of my personal journey towards optimal health. To help you see how I got to this point, and most importantly, to show you how salads can change your life too, let me start with a little personal history.

From Farm to Table

I grew up in the 1960s, the youngest of four children in Tuscumbia, Alabama, and my fondest memories involve food, which was always prepared and presented as an act of love. Whether it was the sweet potato pies my grandmother shipped to me at college with a note telling me to share with my friends, or the candies that the senior ladies at church used to slip me and my siblings (thank you again Miss Lizzie East, Miss Lucy Vinson, and Aunt Mattie Mae), we knew we were loved.

Much of my childhood was spent in and around my grandmother's garden. At the end of each growing season I would spend days at a time standing next to Mama Julia as she canned pear preserves, peach halves, beans, tomatoes, and chow-chow ("cha-cha") pickles. When I wasn't with her, my grandfather, Wiley Mullins, Sr., continued my food education. He was a driver for a produce company, and my brother and I would often ride along with him on his Saturday delivery route. Along the way he would show us how to judge a food's freshness and ripeness and point out how quickly fruits and vegetables can turn. Because of my grandparents, we always ate the best produce in season, at the peak of flavor, right off the vine.

Despite that early beginning, for a long time, my definition of a salad was iceberg lettuce and tomatoes tossed with Miracle Whip. If you had told me then that I could get nutrients from fresh, colorful produce that could help fight cancer and heart disease, improve memory, and enhance eyesight, I wouldn't have believed it.

You see, one of the realities of growing up in a small Southern town is that people oftentimes repeat something over and over again until it seems to become truth. Such is the case of how the people I grew up with viewed sickness, health, and mortality. "You're gonna die with something," or "You're not going before your time," or "God knows best, what's for you, you're going to get." Folks just didn't understand the seriousness of chronic diseases such as hypertension and diabetes. Many were conditioned to believe that sickness was simply inevitable. For most of my life, I too had accepted these statements as gospel, until I realized that we can improve our health and enjoy a better quality of life by making better food and lifestyle choices.

A Concern for Health

Looking back, given my early interest in gardening and the produce business, it's easy to see how natural it was for my career to start with salads. Ironically, the busy, hectic lifestyle that path required eventually set me up for some serious health consequences.

You see, my first job out of college was selling Wish-Bone Salad Dressing to grocery store chains. Eventually, I managed recognizable consumer brands including Vicks NyQuil and Mott's Apple Sauce. Along the way I became so busy with work, I stopped paying attention to my diet or health. As a result, I gained nearly 70 pounds, tipping the scale at close to 300 pounds.

I had always had a big frame, but now I was considered obese. It felt awkward at work, leading discussions about health and wellness issues, and being overweight. It was as if I didn't believe in the marketing message I was trying to deliver. Obesity had become a real issue for me, and my diet and weight were the devils I had to battle.

I knew I had to lose weight and change the way I ate. But I didn't want to forgo the flavors I craved. I decided to start my weight loss plan by returning to what I loved best—fresh produce, clean and simple. I soon began walking the aisles of my local grocery store, buying a wide variety of fruits and vegetables. I would aim for at least one entrée salad a day since that was an easy way to get the five or more servings of fresh fruits and vegetables I needed. An unexpected bonus was that these salads were quick to make—no pots and pans required, no weighing and measuring. I could manage it.

Eating this way, along with some moderate exercise, helped me to shed the pounds. The best part was that I still enjoyed my favorite foods, but prepared in a healthier way.

Over the months that followed, I lost more than 60 pounds by simply incorporating salads into my daily life. And I have kept the weight off for more than 15 years by following the same basic plan.

The Salad Man Takes Action

Inspired by my successful weight loss, I decided to draw on my business experience to help people like me and those in my family and community who were suffering the same fate. At the same time, as a Southerner living in New England, I yearned for the rich taste of sweet potato pies, creamy butter, and salty, smoky pork, but I still wanted to stay in keeping with my new wellness lifestyle.

To meet what I saw as a void in the marketplace, I started my specialty food company, Uncle Wiley's, Inc., and created a line of food products that delivered the flavors I craved, without the fat and cholesterol. They included Wiley's Sweet Potato & Yam Spice, with its cinnamon and nutmeg aroma, Wiley's Corn Boil Seasoning, which offered a buttery taste to corn without the fat or cholesterol, and Wiley's Greens Seasoning, which brought a delicious flavor to collard greens so there was no need to simmer them in pork fat.

And as my business grew, I started to notice customers seemed to have a growing curiosity about salads, so I decided to develop a line of seasonings specifically for salads called Salad Jazz. As I started speaking to church groups, schools, and corporations across the country, spreading the good news about the health and wellness benefits of salads, The Salad Man nickname seemed to fit me more and more. I knew a cookbook wouldn't be far behind.

Inside this Book

The recipes in this book are inspired by a variety of different cultures and regions, including Southern, Southwestern, African-American, Italian, Greek, Mexican, Indian, Chinese, Japanese, Thai, and more. There are a number of salads, however, that I turn to again and again. I call them my Signature Salads because these are the salads that celebrate food from my childhood. They are my comfort food. I have labeled these salads "Salad Man Selects" to make them easy to find.

Beyond cuisine, it was important to me to include a wide range of options, from starter salads and complete salad entrées to dessert salads, so there would be something for practically any menu. After all, *Salad Makes the Meal*. And a fast, easy meal at that—most of these salads can be made in 30 minutes or less, many in 5 minutes or less!

And because it seems to me that so many cookbooks call for fancy ingredients many of us have never heard of before, I decided to stick to basic fruits and vegetables that would be easy to find in local supermarkets, farm stands, and farmers' markets.

Beyond the recipes, you'll also find helpful information on health and wellness, including a guide to eating a nutritional rainbow of fruits and vegetables in Chapter 1. (Choosing fruits and vegetables by color is just one way to maximize their nutritional rewards—see page 3 for more.) I also list the top foods that help to combat chronic illnesses such as heart disease, cancer, and digestive disorders (see page 4), and include details about the recommended daily serving amounts and sizes (see page 2). Chapter 2 offers more practical tips on how to select the best possible produce and how to stock the pantry, and Chapter 3 provides some useful information on equipment, and eating out at salad bars and restaurants. You'll also find "Wiley's Wisdom" scattered throughout the book, helpful tips I've learned over the years to help you store and use what you buy at the peak of freshness, as well as wellness sidebars to help you appreciate all the wonderful nutrients produce has to offer.

Overall, I encourage you to use this book as a road map to healthier eating for yourself and your loved ones. This is not a weight-loss plan, and you are not being asked to give up anything. Rather, if you are adding more salads to your meals (or making them meals in themselves), you are on the road to better health. Consider these nourishing salads a food insurance policy for your body. Eating this way is a reward, one that I hope you'll find as helpful in your life as I have in mine.

—Wiley Mullins
March 2008

Chapter 1
Salad—The Wellness Solution

Years ago, when I decided to make some changes and lose weight, I turned to the fruits and vegetables I've always loved and made them an even more important part of my diet. I enjoyed an entrée salad nearly every day. It was a quick and inexpensive solution for a healthy meal and a great way to enjoy fresh produce.

Along with a little exercise, my strategy worked. But as I lost weight, I also discovered that eating lots of fruits and vegetables wasn't simply a delicious way to cut back on calories. As part of my work in the food business, I started following the research about fruits and vegetables and learned many scientists were finding that people who enjoyed a healthy diet with lots of fruits and vegetables were less likely to face certain chronic diseases, including stroke, heart disease, and some cancers.

Wow! The delicious salad ingredients I loved could actually help me delay—maybe even prevent—some of the nasty chronic health conditions I was all too familiar with from watching friends and family live with them during my childhood.

The recipes in *Salad Makes the Meal* make good use of those ingredients, too, so I thought it best to fill you in on some of the many benefits they can provide. Let's start with some background to highlight what a few salads can do for you.

Science Salutes Salads

Based on results from a number of scientific studies, it seems salad may indeed be the missing piece to the wellness puzzle. Take for instance the research conducted by the University of California, Los Angeles, School of Public Health and the Louisiana State University School of Public Health. They followed more than 17,000 adults over a 6-year period and found:

- Eating salads daily is directly related to higher nutrient levels, which is important for the body's defense against illness.

- Americans do not get enough water-soluble vitamins, such as B-complex vitamins (found in cereal grains, meat, poultry, eggs, fish, dairy, beans, and fresh vegetables) and vitamin C (found in citrus fruits); salads can provide a rich source for these important nutrients.

- People who consume salads regularly are more likely to meet recommended intakes for vitamin C, vitamin B_6, and folic acid.

- Eating a lot of fruits and vegetables has also been associated with lower rates of pre-menopausal cancer and bone loss in women.

- Many salad dressings provide important fats that can help the body better absorb cancer-fighting nutrients such as lycopene and alpha- and beta-carotene.

Even more studies out there confirm that there is a direct relationship between the foods we eat and the overall condition of our bodies. Let's take a closer look at which ones we should target at what amounts.

How Much Is Enough?

The current USDA food pyramid recommends that we consume an average of 3 cups of vegetables and 2 cups of fruit each day, or 9 to 13 servings (to find out more information or calculate your specific recommended daily allowance, visit www.mypyramid.gov). This number might seem hard to reach, but keep in mind that the entrée salads in this book each provide a minimum of 5 servings of fruits and vegetables per person. That's about half of your recommended daily allowance right there. Add a starter, side, or dessert salad to another meal and you've likely hit your mark in an easy and deliciously satisfying way.

Use the following recommended serving sizes to help determine your portion sizes. According to the Food and Drug Administration, one serving is:

- 1 cup raw leafy vegetables, such as lettuce or spinach

- ¼ cup dried fruit, such as raisins or cranberries

- ½ cup raw, cooked, canned, or frozen fruits or vegetables

- 1 medium-size fruit such as an apple, orange, or peach

- ½ cup raw, cooked, frozen, or canned fruits or vegetables

- ½ cup cooked or canned legumes, such as beans or peas

- ¾ cup (6 ounces) 100 percent fruit or vegetable juice

Salads are the fast, easy, and tasty way to combine these servings and achieve the nutritional requirements you need each day. So be sure to consider and provide for salads at every meal (whether they be a starter, entrée, side, or dessert), the same way you might for a starch or protein.

Nature in Living Color

Variety is the key to getting a wide range of nutrients through salads. The more colorful fruits and vegetables you eat each day, the more nutrients and minerals your body enjoys, including fiber, potassium, magnesium, folate, vitamin B$_6$, lycopene, and dozens more. And because many of these plant foods contain important antioxidants that help fight disease at the cellular level, experts now recognize fruits and vegetables offer a lot more health benefits than previously thought. Specifically, antioxidants may play a role in slowing the progression of cancer, heart disease, and age-related diseases by minimizing the damage that a type of rogue molecule called a free radical can create. Because so many of these important antioxidants are found in the same pigments that give plants their distinct color, thinking in terms of what I like to call Nature's Color Wheel makes things easy:

Red fruits and vegetables such as beets, red peppers, pomegranate, red cabbage, grapes, tomatoes, pink grapefruit, cherries, strawberries, raspberries, and watermelon get their color from the plant pigments lycopene and anthocyanin. Lycopene is thought to help reduce risk of several types of cancer and anthocyanin is a powerful antioxidant. These fruits and vegetables are also a good source of fiber and vitamin C, which help promote heart health, lower the risk of certain cancers, and improve overall immunity.

Yellow and orange fruits and vegetables such as corn, squash, carrots, yellow and orange peppers, pineapple, lemons, peaches, nectarines, apricots, and sweet potatoes get their color from the plant pigment carotenoid. These fruits and vegetables also have plenty of fiber and help promote heart health and eye strength, lower the risk of some cancers, and improve overall immunity.

Purple and blue fruits and vegetables such as eggplant, blueberries, black-berries, plums, and raisins are also colored by the plant pigment anthocyanin, which acts as a powerful antioxidant that protects cells from damage. They also contain fiber, vitamins, and phytochemicals that are thought to help reduce the risk of cancer, stroke, and heart disease and improve memory.

Green fruits and vegetables such as lettuces, greens, spinach, celery, asparagus,

Brussels sprouts, zucchini, cabbage, limes, green peppers, and honeydew melon get their color from the plant pigment chlorophyll. They too contain fiber, vitamins, and nutrients that lower the risk of breast, lung, and prostate cancers (among others), help build strong bones and teeth, and improve overall immunity.

White and tan fruits and vegetables such as cauliflower, ginger, garlic, onions, potatoes, turnips, parsnips, mushrooms, and bananas get their color from the plant pigment anthoxanthin. These fruits and vegetables are thought to contain health-promoting phyto-chemicals such as allicin, which may help lower cholesterol levels by slowing cholesterol absorption, lower blood pressure, and reduce the risk of stomach, breast, lung, and other cancers. Some members of the white group, like bananas and potatoes, are also good sources of potassium.

Brown whole grains, legumes, seeds, and nuts contain fiber, vitamins, and nutrients that are thought to help lower cholesterol and reduce the risk of heart disease, certain types of cancer, and diabetes.

Experts advise eating fruits and vegetables each day from all of the groups above. By doing so, you will be taking the necessary preventative steps in the fight against a range of chronic illnesses and diseases. With more than 150 salads to choose from in this book, you can fill your bowl and your body with all of Nature's Color Wheel each and every day.

Foods to Fight Diseases

While I am not a doctor or a dietician, I have reviewed a lot of research on the health benefits of salads. Throughout this book, you will read more about some of the amazing nutrients that make so many of the salad ingredients we enjoy healthful ones. Look for my "A Word about Wellness" sidebars in the recipe section to learn more.

You may also find the charts in the Appendix on page 214 helpful. They reflect top picks among fruits and vegetables based on the studies that show their ability to help fight diseases such as cancer and diabetes, help with heart health, increase immunity, improve vision, and aid against memory loss. For example, those fruits, vegetables, seeds, nuts, grains, and oils rich in antioxidants, fiber, and vitamins (B, C, and E) are known to help protect against certain types of cancer and diabetes, while foods rich in vitamin C and calcium and minerals such as magnesium help strengthen and support both bone and joint health. At a glance I think you'll be able to see why these are the ingredients I've included in my salads whenever possible.

By applying the information in this chapter to your daily food choices, which should include at least one entrée salad daily, you will be taking valuable steps toward a healthier lifestyle.

To make that transition as doable as possible, next we will talk about buying, preparing, and storing produce in relation to the wellness information provided here.

Chapter 2

Power Shopping

I spent much of my Alabama childhood in my Mama Julia's garden, picking, gathering, and eating all of the vegetables my family had planted weeks and months before. We truly valued eating the foods we grew.

Each in its own time during the season, Mama Julia's garden yielded collards, mustard greens, green beans, butter beans, cabbage, turnips, tomatoes, plums, peaches, pears, and green apples. All I needed to do to find the freshest produce was head over to her garden or a nearby neighbor's. And if a garden didn't produce the way we had hoped at spring planting, a vegetable truck would come through town three times a week with delicious offerings grown 2 miles down the road. Hard to imagine these days, but all of the edibles were fresh picked that morning!

Today, few of us have that rich opportunity to eat only what is cultivated in our backyards or grown locally. Instead, we have to sort through all of the many available shopping options and learn how to buy, store, and prepare the ultimate in fresh fruits and vegetables, so that we can produce the best possible salads.

The tips in this chapter will provide you with the tools to help take advantage of purchasing produce seasonally (your tastebuds and wallet will thank you), storing and preparing fruits and vegetables so that you get the finest and freshest ingredients in your salads, and helpful hints for stocking your pantry that make some salads a snap to put together.

Seasonal Produce Guide

With large-scale agriculture and global shipping, many fruits and vegetables are available year-round in supermarkets. But people who seek out the most flavor in fruits and vegetables enjoy them at their peak during specific seasons. You'll find the tastiest peaches and tomatoes in the summer, for example, while mustard greens and sweet potatoes are best during the fall.

Tree-ripened South Carolina peaches are best in late June. The juiciest cantaloupe come from North Carolina in July. Mississippi collard greens are best right around the first frost in November. Use this list as a guide, but be sure to look at your calendar, check with your local farmers, or consult your regional agricultural extension service to find out what is in season where you live.

Farmers' markets are also a wonderful source for produce information. When you're purchasing from the farmer who grew the vegetables, you're guaranteed that the produce is in season. Get to know your local farmers. They are proud of what they do and they share a wide range of information—from upcoming harvests to tasty recipes for fruits or vegetables you may not have tried before.

Here is a general guide to peak-season fruits and vegetables. However, keep in mind that the list will vary, depending on what region of the country you live in.

From Farm to Freezer

Growing up, I used to spend each August helping my Mama Julia with all of her pickling, canning, and preserving. The whole operation would take 3 or 4 days. Our bodies were exhausted by the time we were done, but our spirits swelled with pride in knowing that for the upcoming year, we would be eating the very foods we had grown and preserved with our own hands. Everybody we knew kept pantries stocked with Mason jars filled with pears, peaches, chow-chow pickles, and tomatoes. Miss Nadine King always had the most beautiful green beans, stored whole, in quart-size mason jars. They were almost too pretty to open!

Today, I still preserve the best of summer's harvest, but usually in my freezer, where I can quickly prepare—and stay cool while doing it—and store a wide variety of fresh fruits and vegetables. I make sure to freeze ripe berries (on a cookie tray so they don't stick together) and peaches and nectarines (in sealed freezer bags), which I use for making smoothies and baking. As for vegetables, I find that blanching green peas, corn kernels removed from the cob, lima beans, green beans, and okra in boiling water for 2 to 3 minutes, then draining and freezing them in sealed freezer bags offers a much more pleasing alternative to the same "fresh" vegetables found in my local grocery store come winter. With freezing, I can have the best of summer's bounty to use in my salads all year round.

SUMMER

Apricots
Beans, lima
Beets
Blackberries
Black-eyed peas
Blueberries
Cherries
Chile peppers
Corn
Cucumbers
Eggplant

Figs
Garlic
Green beans
Kiwifruit
Leeks
Lettuce
Mangoes
Melons
Nectarines
Okra
Onions (most varieties)

Peaches
Peas
Peppers
Plums
Raspberries
Squash, yellow
Strawberries
Sugar snap peas
Tomatoes
Watermelon
Zucchini

AUTUMN

Apples
Belgian endive
Brussels sprouts
Cauliflower
Cranberries
Grapes

Greens, collard
Greens, mustard
Mushrooms
Parsnips
Pears
Pomegranates

Potatoes, sweet (yams)
Pumpkin
Quince
Squash, winter
Swiss chard

WINTER

Broccoli
Cabbage
Clementines
Grapefruit
Kale

Leeks
Lemons
Oranges
Pineapple

Radicchio
Rutabagas
Tangerines
Turnips

SPRING

Artichokes
Asparagus
Avocado
Fava beans
Fennel

Fiddlehead ferns
Greens, collard
Onions, Vidalia
Peas
Potatoes, new

Radishes
Rhubarb
Snow peas
Spinach
Watercress

Fruits and Vegetables:
A Guide to Shopping and Storage

In addition to seasonality (see "Seasonal Produce Guide" on page 5), the following are a few things to keep in mind when shopping for fresh fruits and vegetables.

- When selecting produce, make sure to look for solid fruits and vegetables with no signs of cuts, bruises, or mold. Look for good color, firmness to touch, no wilting, and a distinct varietal aroma for peaches, nectarines, melons, and pineapples.

- Remember to buy only as much as you can use within a 3-day period. After that, most produce tends to overripen or spoil.

- If you're buying bagged salad mixes, be sure to check the expiration date on the package and look for the latest date possible to ensure freshness. Be sure to use these salad mixes as soon as possible because sometimes one bad leaf can ruin the whole bag.

- Store melons, tomatoes, peaches, nectarines, avocados, and bananas at room temperature to help with ripening. To speed up the maturing process, place any of these items in a *closed* brown paper bag on your kitchen counter, checking each day for ripeness.

- Don't wash fruits and vegetables until you are ready to use them, as they can quickly turn moldy from moisture.

- Carefully wash fruits and vegetables in cold water before using. Some vegetables, like spinach or leeks, may require a second or even third rinse to remove all of the hidden sand or dirt (see page 47).

- To prevent apples, pears, and artichokes from turning brown when exposed to air, coat the cut fruit or vegetable with a bit of lemon juice.

- Remember to cover and refrigerate any unused portion of produce. Seal tightly in plastic wrap to keep moisture in and allow the items to remain visible so you know what you have on hand.

- Try to visit your local farmers' market as often as possible. The closer the produce is grown to your home, the better it will taste, not having had to be preserved for a cross-country or cross-continent journey.

Stocking the Pantry

Keeping a well-stocked pantry enables you to prepare a delicious, healthy salad in just a few minutes. Many of the salads in this book rely heavily on the ingredients found in the pantry in addition to fresh produce. These are just a few samples of what I like to keep in my kitchen.

Artichoke hearts packed in oil

Beans (rinsed, canned or dried): black beans, cannellini beans, chickpeas, kidney beans, white beans

Dried fruit: apricots, cranberries, currants, raisins

Grains: barley, bulgur, couscous

Honey, natural raw

Maple syrup (grade A)

Mustard: Dijon, whole grain

Nuts: almonds, cashews, pecans, pine nuts, walnuts

Oils: Asian toasted sesame, canola, olive

Olives

Onion family: garlic, leeks, onions, scallions, shallots

Pasta, preferably whole wheat or whole grain

Rice: brown, wild

Salmon, canned, packed in water

Seeds: pumpkin, sesame, sunflower

Soy sauce, reduced-sodium

Tuna, canned white albacore packed in water

Vinegars: apple cider, raspberry, red wine, rice, sherry, tarragon

One last quick note . . . in order to make your salads really sing, I encourage you to use the best-quality oils and vinegars you can find. Be sure to store oils and vinegars in a cool, dark place for up to a year. Nut oils should be refrigerated for up to 6 months. The salads on the pages that follow are all simple to prepare and satisfying to eat. While they don't call for a mile-long list of ingredients, the items they do call for should be the best you can get your hands on. So splurge on that heirloom tomato or aged Balsamic vinegar. Buy extra fresh corn at the farmers' market, remove it from the cob (see page 50), and freeze it in zipper-lock freezer bags for up to 2 months. Try to buy locally grown produce as often as possible. I promise that by taking these extra steps, all of your salads will be successes!

Chapter 3
Salad Notes

Salads are so much more than just lettuce, tomato, and dressing tossed together in a bowl. As The Salad Man, I define the dish as any combination of fruits, vegetables, greens, nuts, seeds, grains, and protein that is served either raw, roasted, wilted, braised, stir-fried, sautéed, or grilled. Salads can be served hot, cold, or any temperature in between.

The creative salads in the next four chapters are unique and enlist all of the ingredients and preparation styles listed above. I challenge you to toss around your own list of ingredients and preparation styles to help broaden my definition!

These salads are presented in the same serving order as courses of a meal. Starter salads can be a first course before a lunch or dinner entrée. Pick the one that best complements what you plan on serving for your main course.

Entrée salads, which come next, can be thought of as lunch or dinner unto themselves. Or, pair them up with a starter salad, side salad, or dessert salad and whole grain crackers or bread for a complete meal that's packed with the recommended daily servings of fruits and vegetables. The entrée salads are arranged by main ingredient category: seafood and fish, chicken and turkey, meat and pork, and vegetarian. There are 90 in all, so you'll have plenty to choose from and never grow bored!

Next up are the varied side salads. They travel well and are the perfect thing to bring to a potluck dinner or fill a brown bag lunch.

Finally we have dessert salads, a distinctive and refreshing way to end a meal. Based mainly on fruits, they won't leave you feeling stuffed and guilty, like many desserts do. You can also serve most of the versatile dessert salads for breakfast. They pair nicely with yogurt and cereal or granola for a healthy and satisfying start to your day.

My goal is to provide you with a wide range of salads for any occasion—from a simple weeknight solo meal to a more formal dinner party or a Sunday brunch. Most of my recipes can easily be doubled or tripled to feed a crowd, or cut down to serve only one or two people.

A quick note about preparing salads: Some of the salads (especially the marinated ones) keep well in the fridge overnight with dressing, but most should be eaten right after they are tossed with dressing. Greens can wilt quickly, releasing liquid which dilutes the taste and texture of the salad. So go ahead and prepare as much as you want in advance, but *toss* only as much as you plan on eating at that meal. Undressed salad can be stored for up to 1 day in a resealable plastic bag lined with dye-free paper towels.

A Word about Greens

In order to get the most vegetable servings possible, most of the salads in this book (aside from dessert) call for some type of salad green, either mixed into the salad or as a bed for a composed salad. Most of us are familiar with iceberg and romaine lettuces, but there is a whole variety of other greens that can add new excitement to the bowl. I hope you will try all of these greens and use them alone or in combination in your salads.

The following list provides details about taste, texture, recommended uses, nutritional aspects, and shelf life of popular salad greens available at most supermarkets.

Popular Salad Greens

LOOSE LEAF LETTUCE
(aka Green Leaf Lettuce)

- Mild, sweet flavor and silky texture

- Good source of vitamin K, niacin, and riboflavin

- Leafy edges are curly and attractive in any salad bowl

- Combines well with sturdier leaf lettuce greens such as romaine and radicchio

- Excellent with vinaigrette dressings

- Shelf life of 3 to 5 days

RED LEAF LETTUCE

- Colorful red leaves that are very tender, sweet, and mild

- Rich in antioxidants

- Good source of beta-carotene, vitamin A, and vitamin B_6
- Shelf life of 3 days

ROMAINE LETTUCE

- Made popular by Caesar salad
- Good source of vitamin C, potassium, folic acid, and lutein
- Leaves are sturdy and firm, creating a very crunchy, crisp texture
- Stands up to creamy and cheese-based dressings
- Shelf life of 5 days

BUTTERHEAD LETTUCE
(aka Bibb or Boston Lettuce)

- Very tender leaves with mild, buttery taste
- Leaf hearts are soft, tender, and sweet while the outer leaves bruise very easily if handled roughly
- Should be combined with sturdier leaf salad greens such as radicchio and romaine for optimal usage
- Partners well with herb flavors
- Shelf life of 2 to 3 days

ICEBERG LETTUCE

- Most popular and readily available salad green
- Crisp, crunchy texture and light to silvery green color
- Lower in nutritional value, given that its water content is more than 90 percent
- Shelf life of 5 days

ARUGULA

- Popular in Italian salads
- Pungent yet pleasing peppery taste and sturdy, bright green color
- Good source of vitamin C, calcium, and vitamin A

- Pairs nicely with citrus and offers nice contrast to salads with avocado or melon
- Shelf life of 3 days

SPINACH

- Most versatile of salad greens; can be served raw, boiled, steamed, or wilted
- Antioxidant-rich, loaded with carotenoids
- Excellent source of iron, folate, vitamin C, vitamin A, and vitamin K
- Goes well with fruit and other salad greens
- Shelf life of 3 to 5 days

DANDELION GREENS

- Strong, tangy, almost nutty flavor
- Excellent source of vitamin A and has some amounts of calcium, vitamin C, and iron
- Goes well with fruit-flavored vinegars and light oils like walnut oil
- Shelf life of 1 to 2 days

BELGIAN ENDIVE

- Bitter green with a taste similar to green chicory
- Leaves are white, almost yellow in places
- Used in salad to add texture and flavor
- Shelf life of 3 to 5 days

RADICCHIO

- Bittersweet taste similar to Belgian endive and escarole
- Deep red and white and very firm
- Used in salad recipes to add texture and flavor
- Can be used as substitute for endive or escarole
- Shelf life of 3 to 5 days

Equipment

Salads are easy to prepare because they don't require a whole lot of fancy and expensive equipment to make them great. Just stock a few good items that can be found in most cooking supply stores, home stores, mass merchandise stores, and some supermarkets. They include:

KNIVES

- **A chef's knife** (8-inch or 10-inch) is indispensable for heavy-duty chopping, cutting, or slicing. I use it for anything from cutting through a whole head of lettuce to slicing chicken breast.

- **A serrated knife** (either bread knife–size or smaller) is good for cutting ingredients with skin, like tomatoes.

- **A paring knife** is also good for small hand work, like coring fruit and peeling skins.

FRUIT AND VEGETABLE PEELERS

- **A traditional peeler** has a sharp end which allows you to dig out any imperfections in whatever you are peeling.

- **A Y-shaped peeler** allows you to peel wider strips, faster. This is especially good for any salads that call for vegetables such as squash to be peeled into wide strips for a decorative appearance.

SALAD SPINNER

A salad spinner is perhaps the most important piece of equipment for making salads. You will use this everyday, so spend a little more money to get a really good one. A sieve set inside a covered plastic container, a spinner dries salad greens and other vegetables by centrifugal force, so that they are crisp, not wilted, in your salad, without causing any bruising to the leaves. Dressings cling better to dry leaves and vegetables, providing a better taste and texture to your salad.

SALAD BOWL

You can use a variety of bowls to toss and present your salads, including ceramic and glass, but I prefer to use a large treated wooden bowl. Lettuce leaves are often delicate, and the wood's texture won't bruise the leaves when tossed. Also, ingredients like onions and vinegar keep their flavor best in wooden bowls. I like using wooden serving utensils for the same reasons. Once salads are tossed in a large bowl, serve them on chilled salad plates or a chilled platter.

Salads Away from Home

Up until now I've talked about the best way to prepare salads at home. Now I'd like to talk a bit about what to look for and avoid when eating salads away from home. Most restaurants, whether they be casual dining, quick serve, fining dining, or fast food, focus more on the appearance and taste of their salads than on their nutritional value. Please don't be fooled. While most salads start out with healthy ingredients, they can also be high in calories and rich in fat from garnishes and dressings. In terms of salad bars, many of them offer such a huge variety to choose from, it's sometimes hard to know which to pick. Here are a few tips for choosing healthy salads on your next outing.

SALAD BARS

- Select salad greens that are whole and haven't been cut, such as mesclun and baby spinach. Cut greens, such as iceberg and romaine, that have been exposed to air allow nutrients like vitamin C to escape.

- Choose items from the salad bar that are fresh, not canned or frozen. Items like red kidney beans are usually from a can which, when not rinsed, can result in high levels of sodium unknowingly added to your salad. Products like previously frozen uncooked green peas are often soggy and can cause your salad to become soggy as well.

- Stay away from meat and fish products on the salad bar unless you can see that they are properly chilled. These high-protein foods are susceptible to spoilage at room temperature.

- Refrain from creamy dressings. They're usually loaded with fat and preservatives and tend to sit heavily on a salad. Instead, use oil and vinegar–based dressings, which are easier to spread lightly.

- It's best to go to a salad bar as close to 11:00 a.m. as possible, since they'll just be putting everything out, which helps ensure freshness in what you choose.

RESTAURANTS

- Always ask for dressing on the side to help limit fat and calories. I prefer vinaigrettes to cream-based dressings.

- Request a freshly cut lemon or lime and some parsley to top off your salad. This will help replace the lost vitamin C that escaped when the items were cut.

- If your entrée salad has meat or fish as an ingredient, request that it be grilled, not fried.

- If you want salad with cheese, like blue cheese or Parmesan, ask for cheese on the side. Chances are your cheeses will be fresher than cheese in a dressing and taste better too!

Now that you have learned about the health benefits of eating salads along with purchasing, storage, and preparation tips, you're ready to begin your salad journey. Enjoy!

Chapter 4
Starter Salads

The starter salad sets the tone of the meal. If you begin with an exciting starter, you've established the overall style for the entire meal, whether formal or informal. I recently served the Tallulah Bankhead Salad (page 27) at a small dinner party. The simple combination of watermelon, raspberries, and feta cheese was a huge hit! Several of my guests insisted that I share the recipe. The best part? The salad got them excited about the remaining elements of the dinner still to come.

Follow these guidelines and your starter salads will be memorable and delicious too:

- The starter salad should be connected to the entrée. As a precursor to your meal, your starter should complement the main course. In fact, it should announce it.

- Most starter salads are typically small and served on individual plates or in bowls. They have only a few ingredients.

- When arranging your salad, incorporate atypical fruit and vegetable combinations on the salad plate to spur immediate interest.

- Keep your starter salad light. It should be refreshing. And the salad plates should always be chilled before adding the salad.

Starter Salads

*Salad Man Selects recipes

Spinach Salad with Strawberries and Buttermilk Dressing

The tartness of buttermilk helps bring out the sweetness of the berries in this refreshing salad. Growing up, we always dipped cornbread in buttermilk. If you have any leftover cornbread, try crumbling it on top of the salad for an extra treat. Feel free to add or substitute your favorite summer fruit—such as peaches, nectarines, plums, or raspberries—for the strawberries.

Serves 4 as a starter

4 cups baby spinach

3 cups quartered, hulled strawberries

12 fresh mint leaves, coarsely chopped

Buttermilk Dressing

⅓ cup sliced almonds

Divide the spinach among four plates. Add the strawberries and sprinkle with the mint. Drizzle the dressing over, garnish with the almonds, and serve.

Per serving: 150 calories, 4 g protein, 21 g carbohydrates, 7 g total fat, 1 g saturated fat, 1 mg cholesterol, 5 g dietary fiber, 309 mg sodium

Buttermilk Dressing

Serves 4

⅓ cup buttermilk

⅓ cup reduced-fat mayonnaise

Juice of ½ lemon

1 tablespoon sugar

Pinch cayenne pepper

Salt and black pepper to taste

2 scallions (white and green parts), chopped

Combine the buttermilk, mayonnaise, lemon juice, sugar, cayenne, and salt and black pepper in a bowl and whisk until well combined. Stir in the scallions.

A WORD ABOUT WELLNESS

Spinach is considered by many researchers and dieticians to be one of the all-time "super foods"—loaded with nutrients, fiber, and phytochemicals. Among its many virtues is the ability to promote bone health because it contains calcium, vitamin D, and vitamin K, which help stabilize and strengthen calcium molecules inside your bones. One cup of fresh spinach delivers 200 percent of your recommended daily value of vitamin K.

Tomato-Mozzarella Towers

It's best to make this salad with perfectly ripe, juicy tomatoes, which taste best with just a little salt and some very good olive oil so as not to obscure their delicate flavor. If, however, you have a yen for this salad when tomatoes are less than perfect, or your olive oil is not so great, you can help the flavor along with a balsamic vinaigrette—use the recipe on page 107, omitting the garlic, and spoon a little over each slice of tomato as you build the towers.

Serves 4 as a starter or light entrée

4 tomatoes, about ½ pound each

Salt and pepper to taste

Extra virgin olive oil

12 to 16 large basil leaves

1 pound fresh mozzarella cheese, the best quality you can find, cut into 12 thin slices

Use a small, sharp knife to cut around and remove the cores from the tomatoes. Working with one tomato at a time, cut a thin slice off the core end so that the tomato will stand easily; this will be the foundation of the tower. Then, still cutting crosswise, cut the tomato into 4 thick slices. Place the bottom slice on a plate.

Sprinkle the bottom slice with salt and pepper and drizzle with a little olive oil (no need to measure, but expect to use from ½ to 1 teaspoon of oil). Place a basil leaf (or 2, if they're small) on top, so that an edge peeks out over the side. Set a round of cheese on top. Set the next tomato slice on top of the cheese, reassembling the tomato. Sprinkle with salt and pepper, add a basil leaf, and top with a piece of cheese. Continue in this same way until you have reassembled the entire tomato. Drizzle olive oil over the top. Repeat to assemble 3 more towers. Serve immediately.

Per serving: 362 calories, 22 g protein, 6 g carbohydrates, 26 g total fat, 16 g saturated fat, 81 mg cholesterol, 2 g dietary fiber, 424 mg sodium

Honeydew Melon with Prosciutto

This classic Italian salad is terrific with any ripe melon, but the colors of the green honeydew against the pink, velvety prosciutto (an Italian cured ham) are particularly nice.

Serves 4 as a starter or light entrée

2½ tablespoons olive oil

1 tablespoon red wine vinegar

1 small shallot, chopped

Salt and pepper to taste

8 slices prosciutto

4 wedges honeydew melon, about 1½" thick, peel sliced off with a large knife (about ½ melon)

4 cups mixed greens

Whisk together the oil, vinegar, shallot, and salt and pepper in a small bowl. Wrap 2 pieces of prosciutto around each melon wedge. Toss the lettuce with about two-thirds of the dressing. Make a bed of lettuce on each of 4 plates. Set a prosciutto-wrapped melon wedge on each, drizzle with the remaining dressing, and serve.

Per serving: 203 calories, 10 g protein, 18 g carbohydrates, 12 g total fat, 2 g saturated fat, 22 mg cholesterol, 3 g dietary fiber, 866 mg sodium

Fried Green Tomato Salad

My grandmother's garden always had a huge amount of tomatoes each summer. There were so many that we would pick a bunch of them once they got big, but were still green, just to try and stay ahead of the bounty of red that was coming up. My grandmother would slice them, coat them in cornmeal, and fry up batches at a time for us. This version still provides the great taste of green tomatoes, but uses much less oil (you'll need to use a nonstick skillet). It's hard to find green tomatoes in the grocery store. Best to pick them from your or a friend's garden, just before they ripen and turn red.

Serves 4 as a starter

1 large egg

¼ cup reduced-fat milk

2 green tomatoes, cored and cut crosswise into ¼"-thick slices (1 pound)

Salt and pepper to taste

¾ cup white or yellow cornmeal

2 tablespoons canola oil, plus more if needed

1 small head iceberg lettuce, quartered (1 pound)

2 red tomatoes, cored and cut crosswise into ¼"-thick slices (1 pound)

Buttermilk Dressing (page 19), made with ¼ cup chopped basil instead of scallions

2 tablespoons sliced fresh mint

Whisk the egg and milk together until well combined. Sprinkle the green tomatoes with salt and pepper, dip in the egg mixture, then dredge in the cornmeal.

Heat the oil in a nonstick skillet over medium-high heat. (The oil should lightly coat the bottom of the pan; add more if needed.) Add the green tomatoes and cook, turning once, until golden brown and crisp, about 5 minutes total. Drain on paper towels.

Place a lettuce wedge on each of 4 plates. Lean the tomato slices against the wedges, alternating green and red slices. Sprinkle the tomatoes with salt and pepper. Drizzle everything with the dressing and top with the mint. Serve immediately.

Per serving: 277 calories, 8 g protein, 37 g carbohydrates, 13 g total fat, 2 g saturated fat, 54 mg cholesterol, 5 g dietary fiber, 400 mg sodium

Warm Asparagus Salad with Shallot Vinaigrette

Roasting asparagus helps strengthen its flavor. When purchasing, look for firm, bright green stalks with tight tips. This salad can be served warm or at room temperature.

Serves 4 as a starter

1 pound asparagus, trimmed

1 tablespoon olive oil

Salt and pepper to taste

Shallot Vinaigrette

Preheat the oven to 425°F. Place the asparagus in one layer in a shallow baking dish. Drizzle on the oil and sprinkle with the salt and pepper. Shake the pan to coat the asparagus. Roast for 5 minutes. Shake the pan to turn the asparagus. Roast for another 5 minutes, or until tender. Transfer to a serving platter, drizzle with the vinaigrette, and serve.

Per serving: *235 calories, 3 g protein, 7 g carbohydrates, 22 g total fat, 3 g saturated fat, 0 mg cholesterol, 2 g dietary fiber, 195 mg sodium*

Shallot Vinaigrette

Serves 4

⅓ cup extra virgin olive oil

2 tablespoons fresh lemon juice

2 tablespoons white wine vinegar

1½ teaspoons Dijon mustard

1 shallot, minced

Salt and pepper to taste

Whisk together all of the ingredients in a small bowl until well combined.

A WORD ABOUT WELLNESS

If you are a woman who is pregnant or trying to become pregnant, reach for foods that contain lots and lots of folate, a B-complex vitamin needed for cell division and DNA synthesis in a fetus. A lack of B-complex vitamins has been associated with some birth defects. Your supermarket is full of folate-rich food: romaine lettuce and spinach, asparagus, broccoli, oranges, avocados, beans and lentils (1 cup of cooked lentils provides 90 percent of the daily requirement), whole grains, and seeds (such as sunflower) are just a few.

Gazpacho Salad

Packed with vegetables, this crunchy salad is ideal for the end of summer when tomatoes, cucumbers, and peppers are abundant in the garden.

Serves 4 as a starter

1 cucumber, peeled and thinly sliced

Salt

2 large tomatoes, cut into ½" wedges

1 green bell pepper, seeded and julienned

3 cups sliced mushrooms

4 scallions (white and green parts), chopped

1 tablespoon chopped fresh parsley

2 teaspoons chopped fresh basil

Spicy Vinaigrette

Pepper to taste

In a colander, run cold water over the cucumbers, then sprinkle with salt. Let the cucumbers drain in the colander for 20 minutes.

Rinse the cucumbers under cold water until all the salt is removed. Pat dry with paper towels and place in a large bowl. Add the tomatoes, bell pepper, mushrooms, scallions, parsley, basil, and vinaigrette. Gently toss until well combined. Season with salt and pepper. Let sit for 10 minutes before serving.

Per serving: 206 calories, 3 g protein, 9 g carbohydrates, 19 g total fat, 3 g saturated fat, 0 mg cholesterol, 3 g dietary fiber, 156 mg sodium

Spicy Vinaigrette

Serves 4

⅓ cup olive oil

3 tablespoons red wine vinegar

1 clove garlic, minced

Pinch cayenne pepper

Salt and pepper to taste

Whisk together all of the ingredients in a small bowl until well combined.

Wiley's Wisdom

Sometimes it's hard to know where to store fresh produce. Should onions be refrigerated? What about bananas? When you are deciding where to store fresh fruits and vegetables, and the temperatures required to keep them fresh, think about the temperature and climate conditions of where they were grown. Store foods like collards, cabbage, lettuces, and carrots in the main part of the refrigerator, where the temperature is around 40°F. These produce items typically grow in cool temperatures. On the other hand, when you purchase tropical fruits like fresh bananas, pineapples, oranges, mangoes, and avocados, don't rush home to put them in the refrigerator. Store them at room temperature to extend their freshness.

Cantaloupe with Lime and Cilantro

Salt and lime bring out the sweetness of virtually any type of melon. Use your favorite here, including honeydew or musk. Cilantro is a fresh herb that looks similar to flat-leaf parsley but has a more intense, bright, citrusy flavor. It is often used in Mexican and Asian cooking. Feel free to use basil instead of cilantro, if you prefer.

Serves 4 as a starter

1 large ripe cantaloupe, seeded, peeled, and cut into bite-size pieces

Juice of 1 lime

3 tablespoons roughly chopped cilantro

Salt to taste

¼ cup chopped cashews

In a large bowl, combine the melon, lime juice, cilantro, and salt and toss. Divide among 4 plates, sprinkle with the cashews, and serve.

Per serving: 121 calories, 3 g protein, 20 g carbohydrates, 4 g total fat, 1 g saturated fat, 0 mg cholesterol, 2 g dietary fiber, 107 mg sodium

Tallulah Bankhead Salad

Tallulah Bankhead, the famous actress from the 1920s and 1930s, was born in Alabama, where she hailed from a prominent political family. This classic Southern salad was named in her honor because watermelons grow in abundance near Bankhead National Forest in the northern part of the state. Some people say that Tallulah was so avant-garde that anything she touched became that much more sophisticated. If so, what better way to pay tribute to her than by dressing up watermelon with raspberries, goat cheese, and mint?

Serves 4 as a starter

4 cups cubed (about 1") seedless watermelon

½ pint raspberries

½ cup crumbled feta cheese

Mint leaves (optional)

Divide the watermelon among 4 shallow bowls or plates and scatter the raspberries and cheese over. Garnish with mint leaves, if desired, and serve.

Per serving: 97 calories, 4 g protein, 16 g carbohydrates, 3 g total fat, 2 g saturated fat, 8 mg cholesterol, 3 g dietary fiber, 137 mg sodium

Cubing Watermelon

To cut uniform cubes, first cut the watermelon into 1"-thick slices and then cut off the rind. Cut the slices into 1" strips, and then cut across the strips to make 1" cubes. Leftover watermelon can be refrigerated in a covered container for up to 3 or 4 days. It's ready to toss into salads or to serve for dessert or a snack.

Thai Zucchini Salad

This salad packs a huge amount of vegetables into each serving. A food processor works very well for chopping the garlic and chiles in the dressing. If you don't have one, use a fork to mash them together. Traditionally, the vegetables are bruised with a mortar and pestle to allow them to absorb the vinaigrette. You can crush the vegetables a few times in the bowl with the butt end of a large knife or a wooden spoon, or even just omit that step entirely, if you prefer.

Serves 4 as a starter

1 pound zucchini, preferably small, washed but not peeled and sliced into long, thin ribbons with a vegetable peeler

2 large carrots, peeled and sliced into long, thin ribbons with a vegetable peeler

¼ pound string beans, trimmed and cut into 1" pieces

6 cloves garlic, minced

2 red Serrano chiles, more if desired, seeded and chopped (wear gloves when handling)

12 to 15 cherry tomatoes

¼ cup unsalted dry roasted peanuts, finely chopped

¼ cup fresh lime juice

3 tablespoons reduced-sodium soy sauce

1½ tablespoons light or dark brown sugar

2 cups shredded green cabbage

2 cups bite-size pieces Boston or Bibb lettuce

Cut the zucchini and carrot ribbons lengthwise into strips and place in a large bowl. Add the beans. Set aside.

Place the garlic and chiles in a food processor and process to a paste, or mash together on a plate with a fork. Add to the vegetables along with the cherry tomatoes. Use the butt end of a knife or a wooden spoon to bruise the vegetables. Add the peanuts, lime juice, soy sauce, and sugar and toss to combine.

To serve, toss together the cabbage and lettuce and divide among 4 plates. Spoon the salad and juices on top and serve.

Per serving: 153 calories, 7 g protein, 24 g carbohydrates, 5 g total fat, 1 g saturated fat, 0 mg cholesterol, 6 g dietary fiber, 482 mg sodium

Wiley's Wisdom

Not all salads feature leafy greens as ingredients. *Crudités* is the name given to a salad where all of the ingredients are crunchy raw vegetables. Produce like carrot and celery sticks, sliced cucumbers, scallions, julienned bell peppers, mushrooms, and broccoli and cauliflower florets is attractive on a large platter with a creamy dressing or vinaigrette for dipping.

Dandelion Greens with Red Onion and Mustard Dressing

Dandelions produce a bitter green that grows wild in early spring. You can pick them yourself (use only the greens from non-pesticide-sprayed plants, and not the yellow flowers!) or look for them at your local farmers' market and in some grocery stores. You can also use any hardy green such as escarole, chicory, or frisée instead of dandelion greens in this salad.

Serves 4 as a starter

4 slices turkey bacon

1 tablespoon Dijon mustard

2 tablespoons cider vinegar

¼ cup olive or canola oil

Salt and pepper to taste

6 cups bite-size pieces dandelion greens

¼ cup sliced red onion

¼ cup golden raisins

In a skillet over medium heat, cook the bacon, turning occasionally, until browned evenly, about 5 minutes total. Drain on paper towels.

Whisk together the mustard and vinegar in a small bowl. Whisk in the oil and season with salt and pepper.

Divide the greens and sliced onion among 4 plates. Drizzle the dressing over. Crumble the bacon over, sprinkle with raisins, and serve.

Per serving: 233 calories, 5 g protein, 17 g carbohydrates, 17 g total fat, 3 g saturated fat, 13 mg cholesterol, 4 g dietary fiber, 402 mg sodium

A WORD ABOUT WELLNESS

Because they tend to be dismissed as garden weeds, dandelion greens are often overlooked by salad eaters. This is a shame, because according to the USDA, the dandelion is one of the top four green vegetables in overall nutritional value. It ranks highest among green vegetables in beta-carotene and has more vitamin A than carrots—14,000 IU per 100 grams versus 11,000 IU. It is also an excellent source of vitamin C, riboflavin, vitamin B$_6$, and thiamin, as well as calcium, copper, manganese, and iron. What's more, dandelion greens have a tangy, slightly bitter flavor that is especially enjoyable in early spring, when the leaves are young (the more mature they are—and the darker—the more suitable they are for cooking). And 1 cup has only 25 calories.

Lentil and Bulgur Salad

This salad can be made the day before and refrigerated. Bring it to room temperature and taste for seasoning before serving. It is delicious with other fruits added, such as grapes, raisins, pineapple, or dried cranberries or apricots.

Serves 4 as a starter or side

⅓ cup green lentils, rinsed well and drained

1 clove garlic, minced

1 cup water

⅔ cup bulgur

⅓ cup walnuts, toasted (see below) and chopped

⅓ cup chopped celery (1 rib)

⅓ cup chopped carrot (1 small)

⅓ cup chopped red bell pepper (¼ pepper)

⅓ cup chopped green bell pepper (¼ pepper)

1 orange, peeled, sliced, seeded, and slices quartered

1 scallion (green and white parts), thinly sliced

3 tablespoons olive oil

2 tablespoons red wine vinegar

Salt and pepper to taste

Place the lentils and garlic in a saucepan and cover with water by 2". Bring to a boil. Reduce the heat and simmer until tender, 15 minutes. Drain well, transfer to a large bowl, and let cool.

Meanwhile, bring the 1 cup water to a boil. Pour the water over the bulgur in a heatproof bowl and let sit until all the water is absorbed, about 15 minutes. Add the bulgur to the lentil mixture along with the walnuts, celery, carrot, red pepper, green pepper, orange, scallion, oil, and vinegar. Stir well and season with salt and pepper. Serve warm or at room temperature.

Per serving: 311 calories, 8 g protein, 35 g carbohydrates, 17 g total fat, 2 g saturated fat, 0 mg cholesterol, 9 g dietary fiber, 97 mg sodium

Toasting Nuts

To toast nuts: Preheat the oven to 375°F. Spread the nuts on a baking sheet and toast in the oven, shaking once or twice, until golden, 7 to 10 minutes. Or just toast in a toaster oven at 375°F, shaking once or twice, 3 to 5 minutes.

Spinach Salad with Pear, Cheddar Cheese, and Applesauce Dressing

Warm applesauce makes a delicious, light, fat-free dressing. You can use any applesauce, but the 4-ounce, single-serve plastic containers are particularly easy (make sure to remove any metal wrapping before heating in the microwave). Use whichever variety pear looks best in the market, including Anjou, Bartlett, Bosc, or Seckel.

Serves 4 as a starter

8 cups baby spinach

2 pears, cored and diced

½ green bell pepper, seeded and diced

2 cups or 4 (4-ounce) individual containers applesauce

2 cups low-fat cottage cheese

1 cup shredded Cheddar cheese

⅓ cup chopped pecans, toasted (see opposite page)

Divide the spinach, pears, and bell pepper among 4 bowls. Warm the applesauce in the microwave for 1 to 2 minutes. Pour the applesauce over the salads. Scoop on the cottage cheese, sprinkle with the Cheddar and pecans, and serve.

Per serving: 352 calories, 22 g protein, 41 g carbohydrates, 15 g total fat, 5 g saturated fat, 30 mg cholesterol, 8 g dietary fiber, 731 mg sodium

Arugula Salad with Grapefruit

Each of the main ingredients in this lovely winter salad has a strong, distinctive flavor. However, when combined they complement each other for a more mellow grouping as the avocado lends a rich, buttery flavor to the tart grapefruit and peppery arugula.

Serves 4 as a starter

6 cups baby arugula

1 large pink or yellow grapefruit, peeled, sectioned, and chopped

1 avocado, halved, pitted, peeled, and cut into 1" dice

2 tablespoons chopped fresh cilantro, or 1 teaspoon dried

Lemon-Honey Dressing (page 36)

Combine all the ingredients in a bowl and toss. Divide among 4 plates and serve.

Per serving: 282 calories, 2 g protein, 17 g carbohydrates, 17 g total fat, 3 g saturated fat, 0 mg cholesterol, 4 g dietary fiber, 85 mg sodium

Wiley's Wisdom

Fruits and vegetables are typically fat free. The avocado is a fruit that is an exception. Its calories and nutrients are derived naturally from the fruit's fat. That fat, however, is monounsaturated fat, the same "good" fat that's found in extra virgin olive oil.

Roasted Beet Salad with Goat Cheese and Walnut Dressing

This classic root vegetable salad makes an elegant first course for a fall or winter dinner party. Try it with a variety of cheeses, including Blue cheese. It's best to let the flavors develop overnight, but if you're short on time you can refrigerate for an hour or more and serve.

Serves 4 as a starter

1½ pounds beets, trimmed, washed, and roasted

½ Vidalia onion, thinly sliced

Walnut Dressing

Butter lettuce leaves

½ cup pecan halves, toasted (see page 30)

1 cup crumbled goat cheese

Slice the beets into ¼" rounds. Place in a sealable container, add the onion and dressing, and gently toss to combine. Refrigerate overnight.

When ready to serve, place the lettuce leaves on 4 plates. Spoon the beet salad on top, garnish with the pecans and goat cheese, and serve.

Per serving: 499 calories, 13 g protein, 27 g carbohydrates, 39 g total fat, 10 g saturated fat, 30 mg cholesterol, 7 g dietary fiber, 916 mg sodium

Walnut Dressing

Serves 4

⅓ cup walnut oil

3 tablespoons balsamic vinegar

1 tablespoon brown sugar

Salt and pepper to taste

Whisk together all of the ingredients in a small bowl until well combined.

Roasting Beets

Preheat the oven to 400°F. Arrange beets in a shallow baking dish and cover with aluminum foil. Roast for 1 hour, or until tender. Let cool. Using a paper towel, rub the beets to remove the skins.

Pomegranate, Pear, and Grapefruit Salad with Raspberry-Pomegranate Vinaigrette

Inside the tough, leathery skin of a pomegranate lie its jewels—hundreds of sweet-sour seeds surrounded by juicy red flesh. Pomegranates have long been considered a significant food in the fight against and prevention of certain types of cancers.

Serves 4 as a starter

4 cups mixed greens

1 pink grapefruit, peeled, seeded, and sectioned

1 pear, peeled, cored, and sliced

⅓ cup pomegranate seeds

Raspberry-Pomegranate Vinaigrette

Combine all of the ingredients in a bowl. Gently toss until well combined.

Per serving: 213 calories, 2 g protein, 24 g carbohydrates, 14 g total fat, 2 g saturated fat, 0 mg cholesterol, 4 g dietary fiber, 89 mg sodium

Raspberry-Pomegranate Vinaigrette

Serves 4

¼ cup olive oil

3 tablespoons pomegranate juice

2 tablespoons raspberry vinegar

1 tablespoon raspberry jam

Salt and pepper to taste

Whisk together all of the ingredients in a small bowl until well combined.

Seeding Pomegranates

To seed a pomegranate, cut around the circumference of the fruit, making sure the knife is inserted only ½" deep. Use the palms of your hands to break the membranes into pieces, then use your fingers to separate the seeds from the membranes. Discard the membrane and skin. Freeze any leftover pomegranate seeds in a single layer on a cookie sheet, then transfer to a sealable freezer bag and store in the freezer for up to 12 months.

Waldorf Salad

This recipe is a healthier update of the famous classic salad first served at the Waldorf-Astoria Hotel in New York City. I've cut out a lot of the heavy mayonnaise and replaced it with a refreshing yogurt-based dressing. Most Waldorf salads call for walnuts, but I prefer pecans for their sweet, toasted, almost maple sugar–like taste that pairs so well with apples. This salad can be served on an apple peel bed, as described below, or, if you prefer, leave the skin on the apples, and serve the salad on lettuce leaves or a bed of greens.

Serves 4 as a starter

4 apples, such as Granny Smith, Braeburn, Gala, or Empire, well washed

Juice of 1 lemon

1 cup chopped celery

1 cup pecans, toasted (see page 30) and chopped

½ cup dried cranberries

½ cup low-fat plain yogurt, preferably Greek

1 tablespoon honey

Slice off the base of each apple in a thin slice and reserve; this will be your base. Then, starting at the base and working in a spiral, use a vegetable peeler to remove the peels from each apple in one piece, if possible (if the peel breaks, just continue peeling). Set each base on a plate. Wrap each peel into a circle about the width of the apple and about 2" high and set on top of a base to make a cup.

Core the apples and chop into small pieces. Place in a mixing bowl and sprinkle with the lemon juice. Add the celery, pecans, and cranberries. In a small bowl, stir together the yogurt and honey. Add to the apple mixture and mix well. Spoon the salad into the apple peel "cups" and serve.

Per serving: 368 calories, 5 g protein, 45 g carbohydrates, 22 g total fat, 2 g saturated fat, 2 mg cholesterol, 8 g dietary fiber, 50 mg sodium

Wiley's Wisdom

Nuts are a rich source of vitamin E, which is essential to the development of strong muscle tissue. Vitamin E is also an important antioxidant that studies suggest aids in the prevention of heart disease. Almonds also contain a substantial amount of potassium, which has been proven to promote heart health. Some nuts, particularly peanuts, may stimulate allergic reactions in some people. If you aren't allergic to nuts, add a handful to your next salad. You'll welcome the added crunch and taste, too!

Pear and Pecan Salad with Lemon-Honey Dressing

You can use any type of ripe pear for this salad, including Bosc, Anjou, Seckel, Bartlett, and Asian. For a more intense flavor, try adding ⅓ cup crumbled blue cheese just before serving.

Serves 4 as a starter

1 pear, cored and thinly sliced

2 tablespoons fresh lemon juice

6 cups romaine lettuce

2 ribs celery, thinly sliced

½ cup chopped pecans, toasted (see page 30)

¼ cup finely chopped red onion

Lemon-Honey Dressing

Place the pear in a bowl, sprinkle with the lemon juice, and toss to coat. Add the lettuce, celery, pecans, and onion and gently toss. Add the dressing, toss until well combined, and serve.

Per serving: 319 calories, 3 g protein, 19 g carbohydrates, 28 g total fat, 3 g saturated fat, 0 mg cholesterol, 5 g dietary fiber, 106 mg sodium

Lemon-Honey Dressing

Serves 4

5 tablespoons olive oil

2 tablespoons fresh lemon juice

1 tablespoon honey

Salt and pepper to taste

Whisk together all of the ingredients in a small bowl until well combined.

Wiley's Wisdom

As a child in small-town Alabama, one of the memorable rites of passage was putting up fresh summer fruits and vegetables. For me, making homemade pear preserves was a highlight. The smell alone was worth all the gathering, washing, and coring of the fruit. That's probably why all of the many varieties of fresh pears are still a favorite today. Not only are pears the ideal energy-boosting snack, they are one of the least likely foods to trigger an allergic reaction. They are also one of the highest fruit sources of fiber. They're simply delicious, too! Remember, the deeper the color of the skin, the sweeter the fruit.

Orange and Celery Salad

This classic salad is traditionally made with fennel (a licorice-tasting autumn and winter vegetable whose root, stalks, and leaves are all edible) rather than celery. If you like, instead of celery use 1 small fennel bulb cut into strips or a combination of the two.

Serves 4 as a starter

4 medium navel oranges, peeled and sliced into thin rounds, juices reserved

2 small ribs celery, cut into 2" sticks (about ½ cup)

⅓ cup thinly sliced red radishes

1 small red bell pepper, seeded and cut into thin slices

Juice of 1 lemon

2 tablespoons olive oil

Salt and pepper to taste

10 black olives, preferably oil-cured

Fresh mint leaves

Arrange the orange slices on a serving platter. Scatter the celery on top, then the radishes, and then the red pepper. Sprinkle with the lemon juice, reserved orange juice, olive oil, and salt and pepper. Arrange the olives on top, scatter a few mint leaves over, and serve.

Per serving: 155 calories, 2 g protein, 22 g carbohydrates, 8 g total fat, 1 g saturated fat, 0 mg cholesterol, 5 g dietary fiber, 200 mg sodium

A WORD ABOUT WELLNESS

When you think of celery, you probably think of the leaf-topped ribs of rabbit food associated with dieting. While it is true that it's a great appetite controller and snack, celery is also an excellent source of phytochemicals: Coumarins protect against cancer by helping to target and eliminate carcinogens and lower blood pressure and may reduce levels of stress, thought to contribute to chronic disease threats. Phthalides help keep arteries that affect blood pressure clear and open. In addition to these and other phytochemicals, celery contains significant amounts of vitamin C, dietary fiber, potassium, folate, and other B vitamins, as well as silicon, which is thought to be important to skeletal and bone health.

Radish and Fennel Salad

This simple but sophisticated salad is wonderful on its own as a starter, or as a side salad alongside grilled chicken or fish. If you can't find fennel, substitute 2 cups of 2" celery sticks.

Serves 4 as a starter or side

¼ cup fresh lemon juice

3 tablespoons canola oil

3 tablespoons olive oil

2 teaspoons chopped fresh chives,
or 1 scallion (white and green parts),
chopped

Salt and pepper to taste

1 fennel bulb, sliced lengthwise into ¼"-thick
strips (about 2 cups)

2 cups sliced radishes

6 cups bite-size pieces red leaf and romaine
lettuces

Whisk together the lemon juice, canola oil, olive oil, chives or scallion, and salt and pepper in a salad bowl until well combined. Add the fennel, radishes, and lettuces. Toss to combine and serve.

Per serving: 218 calories, 2 g protein, 9 g carbohydrates, 21 g total fat, 2 g saturated fat, 0 mg cholesterol, 3 g dietary fiber, 137 mg sodium

Preparing Fennel

Use a large knife to cut off the long stalks close to the top of the bulb. Trim the base. Cut the bulb in half through the root end, and then slice lengthwise.

Pineapple-Edamame Salad with Carrot-Ginger Dressing

Edamame—tender, tasty green soybeans—are sold cooked, both in the shells (often frozen) and shelled and ready to eat, as used in this salad. If you can't find edamame, lima beans make a delicious substitute. The Japanese-inspired dressing will last 3 to 4 weeks in the refrigerator.

Serves 4 as a starter

6 cups Riviera lettuce mix (butter lettuce and radicchio)

1 cup frozen, shelled edamame (soybeans), or lima beans, thawed in the microwave as per package instructions

3 rounds (½"-thick slices) fresh or canned, drained pineapple, coarsely chopped

4 radishes, sliced

Carrot-Ginger Dressing

Combine the lettuce, edamame or lima beans, pineapple, and radishes in a bowl and toss. Divide among 4 bowls. Spoon the dressing over and serve.

Per serving: 263 calories, 7 g protein, 26 g carbohydrates, 16 g total fat, 1 g saturated fat, 0 mg cholesterol, 4 g dietary fiber, 793 mg sodium

Carrot-Ginger Dressing

Serves 4

3 carrots, coarsely chopped

2 shallots, coarsely chopped

1" knob fresh ginger, coarsely chopped, or ½ teaspoon dried ginger

6 tablespoons seasoned rice wine vinegar

6 tablespoons water

3 tablespoons canola oil

2 tablespoons reduced-sodium soy sauce

1 tablespoon sesame oil

Place all ingredients in a blender and blend to puree.

Sesame Oil

Toasted sesame oil is an amber-colored oil made from pressed, toasted sesame seeds. It is not traditionally used for cooking, but rather as a flavoring agent. The flavor is strong, so a little goes a long way. Use it in salad dressings or to season vegetables. Like all oils, sesame oil will go rancid with age; store it in the refrigerator for up to 6 months.

Iceberg Wedges with Blue Cheese–Buttermilk Dressing

Although iceberg lettuce has gotten a bad rap as compared to the more nutritious darker greens, this salad remains a favorite, and with good reason! Nothing beats the crisp crunch that iceberg delivers. And very few lettuces hold up to a thick dressing quite as well. This version of the classic salad bulks up the vegetable servings by adding cherry tomatoes, scallions, and green bell pepper. If you want more texture in the dressing, stir in a little more crumbled blue cheese after pureeing in the food processor.

Serves 4 as a starter

1 large head iceberg lettuce, stem trimmed, cut into 4 wedges

1 pint cherry tomatoes

1 green bell pepper, seeded and cut into strips

Blue Cheese–Buttermilk Dressing

4 slices cooked turkey bacon, crumbled

2 scallions (green and white parts), thinly sliced

Place each wedge of lettuce on a plate. Scatter the tomatoes and pepper around the wedges. Ladle about ½ cup of dressing over each lettuce wedge and distribute the crumbled bacon pieces evenly over the tops. Sprinkle with the scallions and serve.

Per serving: *320 calories, 14 g protein, 20 g carbohydrates, 22 g total fat, 8 g saturated fat, 40 mg cholesterol, 4 g dietary fiber, 1,190 mg sodium*

Blue Cheese–Buttermilk Dressing

Serves 4

1 cup crumbled blue cheese

⅔ cup reduced-fat mayonnaise

⅔ cup buttermilk

Juice of 1 lemon

1 tablespoons canola oil

Salt and pepper to taste

Combine all the ingredients in a food processor and process until smooth, about 10 seconds.

Chapter 5
Entrée Salads

Let your imagination run wild with these 90 main course salads! The sky's the limit—you can assemble colors galore and enjoy pairing many different textures from all the fruits, nuts, grains, vegetables, and proteins that can go into an entrée salad. And the recipes in this section speak for themselves. Regardless of the occasion, whether cooking for yourself or others, these dishes will quickly become fast and easy meal favorites.

Entrée salads allow you the freedom to unleash new food adventures like Warm Catfish Salad with Collards and Watermelon. The larger food portions enable you to taste the richness of flavors like juicy and sweet vine-ripened tomatoes and tart and tangy apples, or the unique flavors and textures of both familiar and unfamiliar salad greens.

Each of these main course salads provides a bountiful collection of wellness in a bowl. The variety within each recipe provides at least five servings of fruits and vegetables per salad—that's more than half the recommended daily allowance! By eating one entrée salad daily, you'll take the necessary steps to help prevent a range of chronic illnesses.

Presentation is of primary importance for entrée salads. Serve up your creations in unusual bowls, plates, or platters to generate additional interest. Use these dishes to create an atmosphere that screams "special." The Hail Caesar Salad is certainly not like any Caesar salad that you've experienced. Most importantly, do not miss the opportunity to showcase the rainbow of color that's abundantly present in fresh produce. Entrée salads are the stars of the stage. Seize the moment!

Seafood

Chicken and Turkey

Beef and Pork

Vegetarian

*Salad Man Selects recipes

Cobb Shrimp Salad

The Cobb salad was believed to have first been served at Hollywood's legendary Brown Derby restaurant. This modern twist replaces the typical chicken or turkey with shrimp and adds sugar snap peas for a crunchier texture. Try grilling the shrimp for a more smoky, caramelized flavor.

Serves 4 as an entrée

- 4 cups butter lettuce
- 2 cups sugar snap peas
- 1 avocado, halved, pitted, peeled, and thinly sliced
- 1 tomato, seeded and cubed
- 1 pound shrimp, cooked

- 2 hard-cooked eggs or egg whites, chopped
- ⅓ cup crumbled blue cheese
- 4 slices bacon or turkey bacon, cooked and crumbled
- Dijon Vinaigrette

Place all of the ingredients in a large bowl and gently toss until well combined.

Per serving: 433 calories, 23 g protein, 11 g carbohydrates, 34 g total fat, 7 g saturated fat, 232 mg cholesterol, 5 g dietary fiber, 637 mg sodium

Dijon Vinaigrette

Serves 4

⅓ cup olive oil

Juice of ½ lemon

1 tablespoon Dijon mustard

Salt and pepper to taste

Whisk together all the ingredients in a small bowl until well combined.

Cooking Shrimp

Many recipes in this chapter call for cooked shrimp. If you're pressed for time, buy pre-cooked shrimp straight from your grocer's fish case. But if you have a few minutes, nothing beats the taste of freshly cooked shrimp. Here are three ways to prepare it.

Sautéed Shrimp

Heat 1 tablespoon oil in a nonstick skillet over medium-high heat. Sprinkle 1 pound peeled and deveined shrimp with salt and pepper to taste and add to the pan. Cook until nicely browned on one side, 2 to 3 minutes. Turn, remove the pan from the heat, and allow the shrimp to cook through with the residual heat in the pan, 2 to 3 minutes longer.

Poached Shrimp

Bring 3" of salted water to a simmer in a small saucepan. Add peeled and deveined shrimp, return to a simmer, and cook until opaque, 3 to 4 minutes.

Grilled Shrimp

Prepare a medium-hot grill or grill pan. Sprinkle peeled and deveined shrimp with salt and pepper to taste. Add the shrimp and grill, turning once, until opaque, 4 to 6 minutes.

Vietnamese Noodle Salad with Shrimp

This salad offers some of the traditional ingredients of Vietnamese cooking such as sesame oil, rice vinegar, and cilantro. If you like a little heat in your salad, try adding 1 chopped fresh red or green jalapeño chile.

Serves 4 as an entrée

1 onion, thinly sliced

White vinegar

6 ounces angel hair pasta

1 pound shrimp in the shell

6 tablespoons rice vinegar

6 tablespoons canola oil

1½ tablespoons sesame oil

3 tablespoons chopped fresh cilantro

2½ tablespoons sugar

Salt and pepper to taste

¾ pound bean sprouts (about 6 cups)

2 cucumbers, peeled, seeded, and cut into 2" strips (⅛" thick)

2 carrots, sliced at an angle ⅛" thick, slices cut into thin strips (or grated)

6 cups shredded green or red cabbage

¼ cup chopped unsalted dry-roasted peanuts

Put the onion in a bowl and add white vinegar to cover. Let stand 15 minutes to temper the bite of the onion. Drain and squeeze dry with paper towels.

Bring a large pot of salted water to a boil. Add the pasta and cook until al dente, about 5 minutes. Drain in a colander.

Bring 3" salted water to a simmer in a small saucepan. Add the shrimp. Return to a simmer and cook until opaque, 3 to 4 minutes. Drain the shrimp, peel, and cut in half lengthwise.

In a large bowl, whisk together the rice vinegar, canola oil, sesame oil, cilantro, sugar, and salt and pepper until well combined. Add the onion, pasta, shrimp, bean sprouts, cucumbers, carrots, and cabbage and toss. Sprinkle with the peanuts and serve.

Per serving: 704 calories, 40 g protein, 67 g carbohydrates, 34 g total fat, 4 g saturated fat, 221 mg cholesterol, 11 g dietary fiber, 386 mg sodium

Wiley's Wisdom

Cucumbers are a delicious salad ingredient, but they can ruin your salad creation if you aren't careful, as they are more than 90 percent water. When they come into contact with certain ingredients, especially salt or sugar, the water is quickly extracted. So be sure to add them to your salad just before serving to avoid excess liquid.

Greek Salad with Shrimp

There's nothing mythical about this salad, only magical! Adding shrimp to the classic Greek salad gives it a quick protein boost. If you prefer, substitute 2 cups cooked, cubed chicken breast.

Serves 4 as an entrée

8 cups bite-size pieces romaine lettuce or mixed greens

2 tomatoes, seeded and diced

1 cucumber, peeled and thinly sliced

1 pound medium shrimp, cooked (see page 45)

½ cup pitted black olives, halved

1 tablespoon chopped fresh mint

1 tablespoon chopped fresh parsley

Lemon-Oregano Dressing (page 143)

3 ounces feta cheese, crumbled

Combine the lettuce, tomatoes, cucumber, shrimp, olives, mint, and parsley in a large bowl. Add the dressing and toss. Divide among 4 plates or bowls, sprinkle with the feta, and serve.

Per serving: 322 calories, 23 g protein, 5 g carbohydrates, 19 g total fat, 4 g saturated fat, 86 mg cholesterol, 2 g dietary fiber, 712 mg sodium

Wiley's Wisdom

Whether it's tender baby spinach or coarse collard greens, washing them oftentimes isn't a simple feat. Whether you have a large abundance of greens or a quantity sufficient for only one person, the task is the same. Place the greens in a large round pan (an old dishpan works well) and cover with cool water. With your hands, move the greens around inside the pan to loosen dirt, debris, or grit. Repeat at least twice, discarding the water both times until clean. Once cleansed, drain the remaining water from the leaves by placing them in a colander or spinning in a salad spinner.

Simple Shrimp Salad with Hot Pepper Dressing

The Hot Pepper Dressing in this salad also acts as a flavorful marinade for the shrimp. If you prefer, the salad can also be spooned into butter lettuce leaves and served as a starter salad for six. Cut down on the jalapeño in the dressing if you like a more mild flavor.

Serves 4 as an entrée

1 pound small to medium shrimp, peeled and deveined

2 tomatoes, seeded and diced

1 yellow bell pepper, seeded and julienned

1 red bell pepper, seeded and julienned

1 cup diced pineapple, drained

Hot Pepper Dressing

Bring a pot of water to a boil. Add the shrimp and cook until opaque, 2 to 3 minutes. Drain and set aside to cool. Once cool, place the shrimp, tomatoes, yellow pepper, red pepper, pineapple, and dressing in a large bowl and gently toss until well combined. Let sit for up to 3 hours before serving.

Per serving: 318 calories, 22 g protein, 14 g carbohydrates, 20 g total fat, 3 g saturated fat, 151 mg cholesterol, 3 g dietary fiber, 226 mg sodium

Hot Pepper Dressing

Serves 4

⅓ cup olive oil

Juice of 1 lime

2 fresh jalapeño chile peppers, minced (wear plastic gloves when handling)

1 clove garlic, minced

Salt and pepper to taste

Whisk together all of the ingredients in a small bowl until well combined. Let stand 10 minutes before using.

Wiley's Wisdom

Entrée salads can be very satisfying as a full meal. The trick is making sure that you have ingredients that are loaded with fiber. Foods that are naturally filled with fiber actually make you feel full without overeating. They also lower the level of "bad" cholesterol in your blood. Always add at least one or two fiber-rich foods to your salad. You'll be more satisfied and you won't have hunger cravings. Excellent fiber sources include beans, pears, apples, and blackberries.

Shrimp and Barley Salad

Quick-cooking barley is a healthy, nutty grain that is available in most supermarkets in the "natural" foods aisle. This fast-cooking version cuts the cooking time from 30 minutes down to 10. If you can't find quick-cooking barley, buy pearl barley, and cook ¾ cup in 1½ cups salted water in a covered pan for about 30 minutes. Barley may also be cooked ahead of time, packed in a zip-top bag, and refrigerated for up to 5 days or frozen for up to 3 months. Soften the barley before eating by heating, covered, in a microwave until warm. Substitute chopped basil or parsley for the cilantro, if you like.

Serves 4 as an entrée

¾ cup quick-cooking barley

Salt and pepper to taste

1 pound medium shrimp, cooked (see page 45)

Cooked kernels from 2 ears corn, or 2 cups frozen corn, thawed in the microwave 1 to 2 minutes

1 red bell pepper, seeded and chopped

1 green bell pepper, seeded and chopped

¼ cup chopped red onion

1 papaya, peeled, seeded, and cut into ½" dice

¼ cup chopped fresh cilantro, or 1 tablespoon dried

⅓ cup olive oil

¼ cup fresh lime juice

6 to 8 cups baby spinach

Bring 1½ cups water to a boil with salt in a saucepan. Add the barley, reduce the heat, and simmer, covered, until the barley is tender, about 10 minutes. Remove from the heat and let stand, covered, 5 minutes.

Drain the barley and transfer to a large bowl. Add the shrimp, corn, red pepper, green pepper, onion, papaya, cilantro, olive oil, and lime juice. Season with salt and pepper.

Divide the spinach among 4 plates. Spoon the salad on top and serve.

Per serving: 547 calories, 36 g protein, 59 g carbohydrates, 21 g total fat, 3 g saturated fat, 229 mg cholesterol, 12 g dietary fiber, 479 mg sodium

Cooking Corn and Removing Kernels

The easiest way to cook corn on the cob is to microwave it, still in its husk, 2 ears at a time: Microwave 3 minutes, then turn the corn, and microwave another 3 to 4 minutes, until the corn is just barely cooked. Let cool a bit, then peel off the husks and stand each ear stem side down in a mixing bowl, holding the pointy top with one hand. Then, with a large knife, cut down along the cob to cut off a few rows of kernels; they'll fall right into the bowl. Give the ear a turn, and cut more rows. Continue until all the kernels have been removed from the ear.

Shrimp and Pinto Bean Salad

Tropical fruits have a particular affinity with lime juice and chili heat, as anyone who is a fan of Caribbean cuisine knows. The acidity of lime and the bitterness of chili powder seem to set off the fruits' exotic, sweet flavor. Mango can easily be replaced with papaya or nectarines.

Serves 4 as an entrée

One 15.5-ounce can pinto beans, drained and rinsed

Hot Pepper Dressing (page 49)

⅓ cup chopped red onion

1 teaspoon ground cumin

Salt and pepper

1 pound medium shrimp, peeled and deveined

Juice of ½ lime

2 teaspoons olive oil

2 teaspoons chili powder

Cooked kernels from 2 ears corn (see opposite page), or 2 cups frozen corn, thawed in the microwave 1 to 2 minutes

1 red bell pepper, seeded and chopped

1 mango, cubed (see page 53)

8 cups arugula or sliced romaine lettuce

½ cup chopped fresh cilantro, or 2 tablespoons dried

Combine the beans, dressing, onion, cumin, and salt and pepper to taste in a large bowl and let marinate while you put together the rest of the salad.

Prepare a medium-hot grill or grill pan. Toss the shrimp with the lime juice, olive oil, chili powder, and salt and pepper to taste and let stand while the grill heats. When the grill is hot, grill the shrimp until opaque, about 3 minutes on each side. (If the shrimp are small and you are grilling outdoors, it's easier to skewer them before grilling.)

Add the corn, red pepper, mango, lettuce, and cilantro to the bowl with the beans and toss. Taste for salt and pepper. Divide the salad among 4 bowls, top each with grilled shrimp, and serve.

Per serving: 493 calories, 36 g protein, 39 g carbohydrates, 23 g total fat, 3 g saturated fat, 229 mg cholesterol, 8 g dietary fiber, 581 mg sodium

Tropical Shrimp Salad

This salad has it all—color and flavor to the max! I urge you to try using mango in your savory dishes. The bright, refreshing taste really stands out in salads, salsas, and relishes. If you like a little heat with your shrimp, add a pinch of cayenne pepper to the dressing, or mince a jalapeño chile into the salad.

Serves 4 as an entrée

1 pound medium shrimp, cooked (see page 45)

4 cups bite-size pieces pineapple

2 mangoes, cut into large dice

1 green bell pepper, seeded and diced

1 red bell pepper, seeded and diced

1 avocado, halved, pitted, peeled, and sliced

3 scallions (white and green parts), chopped

3 tablespoons roughly chopped fresh cilantro

Lime Dressing

8 cups baby spinach, arugula, or watercress, trimmed

¼ cup toasted pumpkin seeds or sunflower seeds

Combine the shrimp, pineapple, mangoes, green pepper, red pepper, avocado, scallions, and cilantro in a large bowl. Add the dressing and toss gently.

Divide the spinach among 4 plates. Divide the salad among the plates, scatter the seeds on top, and serve.

Per serving: *526 calories, 33 g protein, 53 g carbohydrates, 24 g total fat, 3 g saturated fat, 229 mg cholesterol, 11 g dietary fiber, 499 mg sodium*

Lime Dressing

¼ cup olive oil

2 tablespoons fresh lime juice

2 tablespoons white wine vinegar

Salt and pepper to taste

Whisk together all of the ingredients in a small bowl until well combined.

Cutting Mangoes

A mango is oblong, with a thick skin and a wide, flat seed at the center and two rounded "cheeks" of fruit on either side of the seed. Mangoes are very easy to prepare: Stand the fruit on the wider end. Cut the two rounded cheeks off the seed. Set the mango, skin side down, on the cutting board, and score the flesh into cubes, all the way down to the skin. Use your thumbs to press on the skin side, to turn the mango half inside out; the mango cubes will pop out and are easily cut off the skin.

Brown Rice Seafood Salad

The combination of citrus and fresh tarragon, a licorice-favored herb, helps kick up the flavor in this satisfying meal salad. Soaking the onion in cold water helps remove its harshness, effectively sweetening it.

Serves 4 as an entrée

¾ cup brown rice

1¾ cups water

Salt

½ pound bay scallops

½ pound medium shrimp in the shell

One 10-ounce package frozen baby green peas, cooked in the microwave 1–2 minutes until thawed

½ green bell pepper, seeded, thinly sliced, and cut into 1" lengths

½ cup thinly sliced red onion, soaked 30 minutes in cold water and drained

Orange Dressing

2 tablespoons fresh tarragon, chopped, or ½ teaspoon dried

Combine the rice, water, and ¾ teaspoon salt in a saucepan. Bring to a boil, reduce the heat to very low, cover, and simmer until the rice is tender and all the water has been absorbed, 30 to 40 minutes. Let stand off heat for 10 minutes.

Meanwhile, bring 3" salted water to a simmer in a small saucepan. Add the scallops and cook until opaque, about 1 minute (don't wait for the water to return to a simmer before you start timing). Remove with a slotted spoon and set aside. Return the water to a simmer and add the shrimp. Return to a simmer and cook until opaque, 3 to 4 minutes. Drain and peel. Cut the shrimp in half widthwise.

In a large bowl, combine the rice, scallops, shrimp, peas, green pepper, onion, and dressing and toss. Stir in the tarragon. Serve at room temperature or chilled.

Per serving: 465 calories, 28 g protein, 51 g carbohydrates, 16 g total fat, 3 g saturated fat, 105 mg cholesterol, 7 g dietary fiber, 325 mg sodium

Orange Dressing

Serves 4

2 oranges, peeled and divided into sections

¼ cup olive oil

4 teaspoons grated orange zest

¼ cup orange juice

2 teaspoons red wine vinegar

Salt and pepper to taste

In the food processor, combine the orange sections, olive oil, orange zest, orange juice, and vinegar and process to puree the orange well. Season with salt and pepper.

A WORD ABOUT WELLNESS

For healthy adults, the American Heart Association recommends about 1 teaspoon of salt per day, which is equivalent to 2,300 milligrams. Particularly if you have high blood pressure, or are concerned about it, pay attention to the amount of salt you add to home-made salad dressings and to sodium amounts listed on the labels of bottled dressings.

Scallop Ceviche Salad

My father always told me, "If you can't pronounce it at a restaurant, don't order it." I didn't start eating ceviche, a citrus-marinated seafood salad, until after college—I could pronounce it by then! I didn't know what I was missing out on! Traditionally the seafood is cooked only in the acid it marinates in (usually lemon or lime juice). Here the scallops are quickly poached and then tossed with a lime dressing.

Serves 4 as an entrée

Salt and pepper

1 bay leaf

1 pound bay scallops

Juice of 2 limes

3 ripe tomatoes, cut into 1" chunks

1 avocado, halved, pitted, peeled, and cut into bite-size pieces

½ red onion, cut in half through the root end, and then crosswise into very thin slices

¼ cup chopped fresh cilantro, or 2 teaspoons dried

2 tablespoons sliced green olives

2 tablespoons olive oil

1 to 2 tablespoons canned jalapeño chile pepper, chopped (wear plastic gloves when handling)

1 teaspoon crushed (through a garlic press) or chopped garlic

⅛ teaspoon dried oregano

8 cups bite-size pieces curly endive or chicory

Combine 3 cups of water, salt to taste, and the bay leaf in a saucepan and bring to a boil. Add the scallops and cook until opaque, about 1 minute (don't wait for water to return to the boil before you start timing). Drain the scallops in a colander and transfer to a bowl. Discard the bay leaf. Sprinkle the scallops with the lime juice and let cool at least 15 minutes.

When the scallops have cooled, add the tomatoes, avocado, onion, cilantro, olives, olive oil, chiles, garlic, oregano, and salt and pepper to taste and toss gently.

Divide the greens among 4 plates, spoon the salad on top, and serve.

Per serving: 285 calories, 22 g protein, 18 g carbohydrates, 15 g total fat, 2 g saturated fat, 37 mg cholesterol, 8 g dietary fiber, 320 mg sodium

Wiley's Wisdom

Lettuce should always be washed before you use it, particularly if you're using a head of lettuce. Make sure you dry it in a salad spinner before you toss it in a salad. Popular vinaigrette dressing will roll off the lettuce if it remains wet and then settle at the bottom of your salad bowl, quickly ruining your salad.

Marinated Vegetable Salad with Scallops

The marinated vegetables in this salad get more flavorful as they sit. Keep in mind that the salad needs to be made at least 2 hours ahead, but can marinate for as long as 24 hours before serving. For a vegetarian version, try garnishing with crumbled blue cheese instead of scallops.

Serves 4 as an entrée

One 9-ounce package frozen artichoke hearts

1 fennel bulb, trimmed, cut in half through the root end, and sliced lengthwise ½" thick (see page 38)

2 carrots, thinly sliced crosswise at an angle

1½ cups white mushrooms, each halved

2 medium leeks, halved, well washed, trimmed, and chopped

4 shallots, peeled and left whole

2 slices lemon

2 cloves garlic, unpeeled

2 sprigs fresh thyme, or ¼ teaspoon dried

1 bay leaf

4 tablespoons olive oil

1 tablespoon red wine vinegar

Salt and pepper to taste

1 pound bay scallops

8 cups mixed greens

Place the artichokes, fennel, carrots, mushrooms, leeks, shallots, lemon, garlic, thyme, bay leaf, 3 tablespoons of the olive oil, the vinegar, and salt and pepper in a large saucepan. Add water just to cover. Bring to a boil, reduce the heat, and simmer until the vegetables are tender but still have tooth, 15 to 20 minutes. Remove the vegetables to a bowl with a slotted spoon. Boil the cooking liquid until reduced to slightly less than ¾ cup. Discard the bay leaf and thyme sprigs. Pour the liquid over the vegetables, and stir gently. Let cool to room temperature, at least 2 hours.

Bring 3" of lightly salted water to a simmer in a small saucepan. Add the scallops and cook until opaque, about 1 minute (don't wait for water to return to the boil before you start timing). Drain and set aside.

Divide the greens among 4 plates. Use a slotted spoon to spoon the marinated vegetables on top of the greens. Top with the scallops. Drizzle with a little of the marinating liquid, then the remaining 1 tablespoon olive oil, and serve.

Per serving: 354 calories, 26 g protein, 31 g carbohydrates, 16 g total fat, 2 g saturated fat, 37 mg cholesterol, 10 g dietary fiber, 388 mg sodium

Cleaning Leeks

Trim the root end of the leek and cut off the tough green ends, cutting down to the light green part. Cut the leek in half lengthwise, and rinse well under cold running water, gently pulling open the leaves to expose and remove any sand.

Mussel and New Potato Salad

Steamed mussels have become a favorite of mine since moving to New England. Serve this elegant salad with a good crusty loaf of whole grain bread to help sop up all of the delicious juices.

Serves 4 as an entrée

1 cup dry white wine

3 scallions (green and white parts), cut into 1" lengths

3 parsley sprigs

2 bay leaves

4 pounds mussels, washed in cold water and debearded if necessary

1 pound new potatoes, peeled and cut into 1" cubes

Red Wine Dressing

8 cups bite-size pieces of mixed greens

Bring the wine, scallions, parsley, and bay leaves to a boil in a large pot and simmer for 3 minutes. Add the mussels, cover, and cook, shaking the pot from time to time, until the shells have opened, about 5 minutes. Remove the mussels from the liquid with a skimmer or slotted spoon. Shell the mussels, discarding any that haven't opened. Measure out 6 tablespoons of the cooking broth and reserve. Discard the remaining broth.

While the mussels are cooking, cover the potatoes in a saucepan with cold salted water. Bring to a boil, reduce the heat, and simmer until tender, 4 to 5 minutes. Drain in a colander. Transfer to a bowl and sprinkle with the reserved mussel broth. Add the mussels and dressing and toss until well combined.

Divide the greens among 4 plates, top with the salad, and serve.

Per serving: 442 calories, 31 g protein, 18 g carbohydrates, 26 g total fat, 4 g saturated fat, 64 mg cholesterol, 5 g dietary fiber, 758 mg sodium

Red Wine Dressing

Serves 4

6 tablespoons olive oil

1½ tablespoons red wine vinegar

Salt and pepper to taste

Whisk together all of the ingredients in a small bowl until well combined.

Preparing Mussels

While most cultivated mussels are very clean and have very little in the way of "beards"—the steel wool-like bits that protrude from the shells and must be removed before cooking—they must still be washed under cold running water to help remove any grit. Be sure to discard any mussels that are open. (Try inserting a knife into the open mussels—if the shells close, the mussels are okay to use.) For any of the mussels that still have the beard attached, scrape and pull off with a small knife.

Squash Salad with Salmon Teriyaki

Layered with wide, thin strips of zucchini and summer squash, the base of this salad is similar to pappardelle pasta. It makes the perfect entrée for a dinner party.

Serves 4 as an entrée

½ pound asparagus, trimmed

1 tablespoon olive oil

Salt to taste

3 tablespoons reduced-sodium teriyaki sauce

1 pound salmon fillet with skin

1 zucchini, cut lengthwise with a Y-shaped vegetable peeler into wide strips (about 1½ cups)

1 summer squash, cut lengthwise with a Y-shaped vegetable peeler into wide strips (about 1½ cups; see Note)

1 tablespoon rice wine vinegar

Preheat the broiler and place an oven rack 3" to 4" from the broiling element.

Brush the asparagus with the olive oil and sprinkle with salt. Place on a baking sheet or broiling pan. Sprinkle 1 tablespoon of the teriyaki sauce on the flesh side of the salmon and lay on the baking sheet or broiling pan, flesh side up, next to the asparagus. Broil the asparagus and salmon for 2 minutes. Turn the salmon and sprinkle the skin side with 1 tablespoon teriyaki sauce. Broil until the salmon is firm and still translucent in the center, about 2 minutes longer, depending on the thickness of the fillet.

Remove the salmon from the baking sheet or broiling pan. Turn the asparagus, return it to the broiler, and cook until lightly browned, 4 or 5 minutes longer.

Arrange the zucchini and summer squash strips in the center of a serving platter. Sprinkle with the remaining 1 tablespoon teriyaki sauce and the rice wine vinegar. Remove the skin from the salmon and use a fork to flake. Add the salmon to the squash; toss gently. Arrange the asparagus spears on either side of the salad and serve.

Per serving: 228 calories, 25 g protein, 8 g carbohydrates, 11 g total fat, 2 g saturated fat, 62 mg cholesterol, 2 g dietary fiber, 324 mg sodium

Note: Yellow squash contains a lot of large seeds, which make the texture spongy. You can avoid the seeds by peeling off strips until you begin to see seeds, then turning the squash over and peeling the other side until you encounter seeds. Peel the remaining 2 sides and discard the center.

Salmon Salad with Cherry Tomatoes and Lemon

My Aunt Ollie used to make breaded and fried salmon croquettes. This salad is a much healthier way to serve salmon, with its wonderful fresh, clean taste. The radishes add a peppery crunch and a bit of a kick to it. If you don't want to buy a large jar of olives, most supermarkets have a deli section where you can buy small amounts of different types of olives.

Serves 4 as an entrée

1 pound salmon fillet, with or without skin

Salt and pepper to taste

1 tablespoon canola oil

6 tablespoons olive oil

3 tablespoons fresh lemon juice

3 tablespoons chopped fresh basil, or
   1 teaspoon dried

1 clove garlic, crushed in a press or finely
   minced

1 cup halved cherry tomatoes

1 cup sliced radishes

¼ cup black olives such as Kalamata or
   oil-cured, pitted and coarsely chopped

½ cup pomegranate seeds

4 cups slivered cabbage

4 cups sliced romaine lettuce

Sprinkle the salmon with salt and pepper. Heat the canola oil in a nonstick skillet over medium heat. Add the salmon and cook, turning once, until the salmon is firm but still translucent in the center, about 10 minutes. Let cool.

Combine the olive oil, lemon juice, basil, and garlic in a bowl and whisk until well combined. Season with salt and pepper.

Remove the skin from the salmon, if any. Use a fork to flake the flesh into the bowl with the dressing. Add the tomatoes, radishes, olives, and pomegranate seeds to mix.

In another bowl, toss together the cabbage and lettuce. Divide among 4 plates, spoon the salmon salad with its juices on top, and serve.

Per serving: 451 calories, 25 g protein, 17 g carbohydrates, 32 g total fat, 4 g saturated fat, 62 mg cholesterol, 4 g dietary fiber, 216 mg sodium

Wiley's Wisdom

Think flavor, when selecting the appropriate oil for homemade salad dressings. Most oils that are used for frying or sautéing, such as vegetable, corn, and peanut oil, lack flavor. The ideal oils for salad dressings are olive oil (extra virgin), Asian toasted sesame oil, and walnut oil.

Salmon and Brown Rice Salad

This is an ideal summer salad, as you can use pretty much whatever fruits and vegetables you like. For example, add red or green bell peppers, or mushrooms; switch the peach to a plum, nectarine, or apricots; or use shrimp or chicken instead of salmon.

Serves 6 as an entrée

¾ cup brown rice

1¾ cups water

Salt and pepper

1 tablespoon olive oil

1 pound salmon fillet with skin

1 peach, pitted and cut into bite-size pieces

2 small zucchini (about ⅔ pound), trimmed and cut into small (⅓") dice

2 ripe tomatoes, cut into 1" dice

1 avocado, halved, pitted, peeled, and cut into bite-size pieces

1 cucumber, peeled and cut into small (⅓") dice

2 scallions (white and green parts), thinly sliced

¼ cup roughly chopped fresh parsley

¼ cup roughly chopped fresh basil

Lemon-Dijon Vinaigrette

6 cups bite-size pieces butter or Boston lettuce

1 lemon, cut into wedges

Combine the rice, water, and salt to taste in a saucepan. Bring to a boil and reduce the heat to very low. Cover and simmer until the rice is tender and all the water has been absorbed, 30 to 40 minutes. Let stand off heat for 10 minutes.

Preheat the broiler and place an oven rack 6" from the broiling element. Line a baking sheet with aluminum foil and drizzle a small area with the olive oil. Rub the flesh side of the salmon in the oil and set on the lightly oiled foil flesh side up. Sprinkle with salt and pepper to taste. Broil until the salmon is firm but still translucent in the center, 5 to 8 minutes, depending on the thickness of the fillet. Remove the skin and use a fork to divide the salmon into six roughly even pieces.

Gently stir the peach, zucchini, tomatoes, avocado, cucumber, scallions, parsley, and basil into the rice. Add the dressing and stir. Taste for salt and pepper.

Line a shallow serving bowl with the lettuce. Spoon the salad into the bowl and arrange the salmon on top. Serve with the lemon wedges.

Per serving: 614 calories, 30 g protein, 44 g carbohydrates, 37 g total fat, 5 g saturated fat, 62 mg cholesterol, 8 g dietary fiber, 270 mg sodium

Lemon-Dijon Vinaigrette

Serves 6

⅓ cup olive oil

2 tablespoons fresh lemon juice

2 tablespoons white wine vinegar

2 shallots, minced

1½ teaspoons Dijon mustard

Salt and pepper to taste

Whisk together all of the ingredients in a small bowl until well combined.

Wiley's Wisdom

Most Americans consume fewer than 3 to 4 servings of produce daily. This is roughly 33 percent of the recommended 9 to 13 servings daily. By eating one entrée salad daily, you can more than double your vitamin and mineral intake with just one meal.

Warm Catfish Salad with Collards and Watermelon

For years I thought the only way to enjoy catfish was fried in a golden cornmeal crust. However, once I experienced this salad I realized that the mild and versatile taste of catfish really comes through without all that breading and frying. If you can't find catfish, feel free to use any mild white, flaky fish fillet, or even salmon. Cooking the collards in a little oil preserves the pleasantly bitter flavor of the green, which tastes terrific with watermelon. Once the watermelon has been dressed, it will begin to give off juice, so the salad should be served immediately.

Serves 4 as an entrée

2 cloves garlic, sliced

2 tablespoons olive or canola oil

2 medium bunches collard greens
   (1¼–1½ pounds), stemmed and shredded

½ cup water

Salt and black pepper to taste

1 pound catfish fillet

Cayenne pepper to taste

6 cups cubed (about ¾") seedless watermelon
   (see page 27)

½ cup sliced red onion

2 scallions (white and green parts), thinly sliced

¾ cup sliced (on the bias) celery

Bright Lemon Dressing

Combine the garlic and 1 tablespoon of the oil in a large skillet (preferably nonstick). Set the skillet over medium-low heat and cook until the garlic sizzles but does not brown, 1 to 2 minutes. Add the greens, water, and ¼ teaspoon salt and stir. Cover and cook until the collards are tender but still chewy, 10 to 15 minutes, depending on the age of the greens. (If the water evaporates before the greens are cooked, add a little more.) Transfer to a bowl or plate to cool.

Preheat the broiler and place the oven rack 2" to 3" from the broiler element. Lay the fillets on a lightly greased baking sheet. Sprinkle generously with salt and pepper and more sparingly with cayenne (or to taste). Drizzle with the remaining 1 tablespoon oil. Broil the fish until barely cooked through and still a little translucent in the center, 3 to 5 minutes, depending on your oven. Divide into 4 portions and set aside.

Combine the collards, watermelon, onion, scallions, and celery in a large bowl. Add about one-half of the dressing and toss gently. Divide the salad among 4 plates and top with the catfish. Drizzle the remaining dressing over the fish and salad and serve.

Per serving: 460 calories, 23 g protein, 29 g carbohydrates, 30 g total fat, 5 g saturated fat, 53 mg cholesterol, 7 g dietary fiber, 257 mg sodium

Bright Lemon Dressing

Serves 4

¼ cup olive oil

3 tablespoons fresh lemon juice

1 tablespoon red wine vinegar

Salt and pepper to taste

Whisk together all of the ingredients in a small bowl until well combined.

A WORD ABOUT WELLNESS

Collard greens are members of the cruciferous family, along with broccoli, cabbage, kale, turnip greens, kohlrabi, and watercress. Cruciferous vegetables have high levels of cancer-fighting phytochemicals called isothiocyanates, which neutralize carcinogens and speed up their elimination from the body. One of collards' sulfur-containing phytochemicals—sulforaphane—may prevent breast and ovarian cancers. Collard greens also contain the carotenoids lutein and zeaxanthin, which protect the eyes from free-radical damage that could eventually cause blindness. Of particular interest to those of you hoping to improve your bone health, a cup of collard greens has almost the same amount of calcium as an 8-ounce glass of milk, making it a valuable, dairy-free alternative source of calcium.

Tuna-Stuffed Tomatoes

This salad is perfect for a summer luncheon. It's both filling and attractive and can be made quickly for any last-minute guests who drop by.

Serves 4 as an entrée

4 medium, ripe tomatoes (about 2 pounds)

Salt

Two 6-ounce cans white albacore tuna packed in water, drained

¼ cup chopped celery

¼ cup diced green pepper

3 tablespoons minced onion

3 tablespoons chopped fresh dill, or 2 teaspoons dried

2 tablespoons reduced-fat mayonnaise

Juice of ½ lemon

¼ teaspoon pepper

4 large cup-shaped lettuce leaves

Red Wine Dressing (page 59)

Slice the top off of each tomato; scoop out and discard the pulp. Sprinkle the insides with salt to taste. In a large bowl, combine the tuna, celery, green pepper, onion, dill, mayonnaise, lemon juice, and pepper and stir to mix. Fill the tomatoes with the tuna mixture. Place each tomato on a lettuce leaf, drizzle with the dressing, and serve.

Per serving: 311 calories, 10 g protein, 13 g carbohydrates, 24 g total fat, 4 g saturated fat, 318 mg cholesterol, 1 g dietary fiber, 729 mg sodium

Variation: Tomatoes Stuffed with Deviled Egg Salad

Serves 4 as an entrée

¼ cup canola oil

¼ cup reduced-fat mayonnaise

4 teaspoons Dijon mustard

2 teaspoons chopped red onion

Several dashes Tabasco sauce

6 hard-cooked eggs, coarsely chopped

1 cup chopped homemade (see page 181) or jarred roasted red peppers

2 ribs celery, chopped

¼ cup sweet pickle relish

Salt and pepper to taste

In a medium bowl, whisk together the oil, mayonnaise, mustard, onion, and Tabasco until combined. Add the eggs, red peppers, celery, relish, and salt and pepper and fold together.

Fill 4 hollowed-out tomatoes with the egg salad and arrange on lettuce leaves.

Per serving: 356 calories, 12 g protein, 25 g carbohydrates, 25 g total fat, 4 g saturated fat, 318 mg cholesterol, 3 g dietary fiber, 703 mg sodium

Wiley's Wisdom

Have you ever purchased a tomato in the middle of the winter that looked like it was vine-ripened but lacked flavor and taste? Chances are that your tomato was genetically altered. The best way to avoid genetically manipulated foods is to purchase foods seasonally from farmers' markets that feature locally grown produce. You can also grow delicious tomatoes in pots on your patio or porch.

Tuna Salad with Grilled Vegetables

Who says tuna can't be dressed up? This salad is a variation of the traditional French *Salade Niçoise*, which traditionally calls for hard-cooked eggs and green beans (feel free to add them here). It's very pretty presented family style on a large platter, but can just as easily be tossed all together in a bowl, if you like.

Serves 4 as an entrée

6 new potatoes

Pesto Dressing (page 133)

1 tablespoon water

One 6-ounce can albacore tuna packed in water, drained

½ pound small summer squash (zucchini and/or yellow squash), trimmed and cut in half lengthwise

1 eggplant, about ¾ pound, trimmed and cut into ½"-thick rounds

1 red bell pepper, seeded and quartered

4 scallions (white and green parts), trimmed

2 tablespoons olive oil, for brushing

Salt and pepper to taste

Juice of ½ lemon

8 cups bite-size pieces Boston lettuce or other mixed lettuces

1 large tomato, cut into eighths

One 9-ounce package frozen lima beans, steamed or cooked in a microwave until warm

6 radishes, sliced

1 cup pitted black olives

Put the potatoes in a saucepan and add cold salted water just to cover. Bring to a simmer and cook until tender when pierced with the tip of a small knife, 20 to 25 minutes. Drain.

Stir together the dressing and water in a bowl. Add the tuna and stir to break up and coat with the dressing. Let the tuna marinate while you prepare the rest of the vegetables.

Prepare a medium-hot grill or grill pan. Place the squash, eggplant rounds, red pepper, and scallions in a single layer on a baking sheet. Brush with some of the olive oil and sprinkle with salt and pepper. Working in batches, place the vegetables on the grill, oiled side down. Brush with more oil and sprinkle with salt and pepper. Grill until softened and well browned, about 5 minutes each side for the squash; 3 to 5 minutes each side for the eggplant; 3 to 4 minutes each side for the pepper; and 2 to 3 minutes each side for the scallions. As they finish cooking, transfer to a plate. Cut the squash into 3" lengths, quarter the eggplant rounds, and cut the scallions in half. Squeeze the lemon over.

Make a bed of lettuce on a large platter. Arrange the potatoes, tuna, grilled vegetables, tomato, lima beans, and radishes neatly on top in separate piles. Scatter the olives on top, drizzle with any dressing from the tuna bowl, and serve.

Per serving: 535 calories, 25 g protein, 42 g carbohydrates, 32 g total fat, 5 g saturated fat, 18 mg cholesterol, 18 g dietary fiber, 657 mg sodium

Pasta Shells with Tuna and Roasted Red Bell Pepper Dressing

This salad is a snap to prepare. The vegetables get tossed into the cooking water with the pasta and then drained and tossed with a flavorful red pepper dressing. If you like, try it with 1 cup of diced mango instead of the grapes.

Serves 4 as an entrée

½ pound pasta shells, preferably whole grain

1 head broccoli, cut into florets

¼ pound green beans, halved

One 7½-ounce jar roasted red pepper, drained, or 1 homemade roasted pepper (see page 181)

4 tablespoons olive oil

1 tablespoon balsamic vinegar

Salt and pepper to taste

One 6-ounce can solid white albacore tuna packed in water, drained

1 carrot, grated

1 cup halved red or green seedless grapes

¼ cup chopped red onion

¼ cup pecans, toasted (see page 30) and chopped

¼ cup roughly chopped fresh basil, parsley, or cilantro, or 2 teaspoons dried

8 cups bite-size pieces red leaf lettuce

Bring a large pot of water to a boil. Add the pasta and cook for the number of minutes suggested on the package, but 2 minutes before the pasta is cooked add the broccoli and green beans. Drain the pasta and vegetables in a colander; refresh under cold running water.

While the pasta cooks, combine the red pepper, 3 tablespoons of the oil, and the vinegar in a blender and blend until smooth. Scrape into a large bowl and season with salt and pepper. Add the tuna, break it up with a spoon, and let marinate in the dressing.

Transfer the drained pasta mixture to the bowl with the tuna and dressing. Add the carrot, grapes, onion, pecans, and herb and toss. Taste for seasoning. In another bowl, toss the lettuce with the remaining 1 tablespoon oil and season lightly with salt and pepper.

Make a bed of lettuce on each of 4 plates, spoon the pasta mixture on top, and serve.

Per serving: 559 calories, 25 g protein, 70 g carbohydrates, 22 g total fat, 3 g saturated fat, 18 mg cholesterol, 10 g dietary fiber, 447 mg sodium

Tuna Salad with Watermelon and Tomato

This salad offers an ideal fruit and vegetable pairing. The acid in the tomatoes complements the sweetness in the watermelon. You can use any variety of seedless watermelon, including yellow, or try a combination of red and yellow watermelon for a colorful presentation.

Serves 4 as an entrée

2 beefsteak or large ripe tomatoes, cut in half through the wide middle, squeezed gently over the sink to remove seeds, and cut into 1" dice (about 3 cups)

3 cups seedless cubed (about 1") watermelon (see page 27)

1 cucumber, peeled, quartered lengthwise, and cut into 1" pieces (about 1½ cups)

Cooked kernels from 1 ear corn (see page 50), or 1 cup frozen corn, thawed in the microwave 1 to 2 minutes

⅓ cup crumbled feta cheese

¼ cup chopped red onion

1 tablespoon chopped fresh mint, or ½ teaspoon dried

Red Wine Dressing

Salt and pepper to taste

8 cups bite-size pieces romaine lettuce

One 6-ounce can solid white albacore tuna packed in water, drained

In a large bowl, gently toss together the tomatoes, watermelon, cucumber, corn, cheese, onion, and mint. Add about half of the dressing and toss gently to coat. Add salt and pepper.

Divide the lettuce among 4 plates and top with the salad. Divide the tuna among the salads, drizzle with the remaining dressing, and serve.

Per serving: 212 calories, 17 g protein, 27 g carbohydrates, 6 g total fat, 3 g saturated fat, 29 mg cholesterol, 5 g dietary fiber, 396 mg sodium

Red Wine Dressing with a Kick

Serves 4

¼ cup olive oil

2 tablespoons red wine vinegar

Salt and pepper to taste

Dash hot pepper sauce, or to taste

Whisk together all of the ingredients in a small bowl until well combined.

A WORD ABOUT WELLNESS

Ninety-two percent of watermelon is water, making it the perfect food for weight loss. Why? Because, as researchers confirm, food that contains a high volume of water is absorbed more slowly and stays longer in your digestive system, delaying hunger and discouraging overeating. But water is only part of its story. Watermelon is also low in calories and full of vitamin A and lycopene, the same carotenoid in tomatoes that may help to reduce prostate, lung, and liver cancer risks. To get the most nutritional benefit from a watermelon, though, don't refrigerate it until after you have cut into it (it will last as long as 4 weeks on the counter). While it is at room temperature, the fruit's lycopene levels are about 20 percent higher than if the watermelon is chilled, according to the USDA.

Tuna and White Bean Salad

This salad is also delicious served in a whole wheat pita or spread on some slices of grilled, crusty whole grain bread.

Serves 4 as an entrée

8 cups shredded iceberg lettuce

One 15-ounce can white beans, such as cannellini, drained and rinsed under cold water

One 6-ounce can albacore tuna packed in water, drained

1 tart apple, such as Granny Smith, cored but not peeled, and cut into chunks

2 small ribs celery, diced (about ½ cup)

¼ cup chopped red onion

¼ cup chopped fresh parsley, or 2 teaspoons dried

1 tablespoon fresh sage, or ½ teaspoon dried

6 tablespoons olive oil

¼ cup red wine vinegar

Salt and pepper to taste

In a large bowl combine the lettuce, beans, tuna, apple, celery, onion, parsley, and sage. Mix together the oil, vinegar, and salt and pepper in a small bowl until well combined. Drizzle over the salad, toss to combine, and serve.

Per serving: 363 calories, 17 g protein, 26 g carbohydrates, 22 g total fat, 3 g saturated fat, 18 mg cholesterol, 6 g dietary fiber, 267 mg sodium

Oven-Fried Chicken Salad

Growing up, every family in town always had the same meal on the table for Sunday dinner—fried chicken, potato salad, green beans, macaroni and cheese, brown-and-serve rolls, sweet tea, and lemon icebox pie. This salad reminds me of Sunday dinners, only this chicken's a lot healthier. A cornflake coating is used on the chicken to create a nice, crisp texture in the oven, avoiding having to fry anything.

Serves 4 as an entrée

½ pound chicken tenders (6 tenders), each cut in half lengthwise

Salt and pepper

¼ cup all-purpose flour

1 large egg, lightly beaten

1½ cups cornflake cereal, crushed to small crumbs

8 cups chopped romaine lettuce

1 cucumber, peeled and sliced

2 small carrots, sliced

1 large tomato, cored and diced

Cooked kernels from 1 ear of corn (see page 50), or 1 cup frozen corn, thawed in the microwave 1 to 2 minutes

Honey-Buttermilk Dressing

Preheat the oven to 400°F. Season the chicken with salt and pepper. Dredge in the flour, then dip in the egg and coat with the cornflakes. Transfer to a nonstick baking sheet. Bake until the crust is browned and crisp and the chicken cooked through, about 20 minutes. Let cool.

In a large bowl, toss the lettuce, cucumber, carrots, tomato, and corn with the dressing. Divide the salad among 4 serving plates, top each with 3 pieces of chicken, and serve.

Per serving: 247 calories, 21 g protein, 38 g carbohydrates, 3 g total fat, 1 g saturated fat, 88 mg cholesterol, 5 g dietary fiber, 337 mg sodium

Honey-Buttermilk Dressing

Serves 4

½ cup buttermilk

¼ cup low-fat plain yogurt, preferably Greek

2 tablespoons cider vinegar

1 tablespoon honey

Salt and pepper to taste

Whisk together all of the ingredients in a small bowl until well combined.

Curried Chicken Salad with Mushrooms and Brown Rice

The combination of chicken, brown rice, and vegetables makes this salad a complete and satisfying meal. If you'd like to serve the salad in a sandwich, omit the rice and cut down on the dressing.

Serves 4 as an entrée

2 tablespoons olive oil

2 cups sliced mushrooms

2 cups cubed cooked chicken breast

2 cups cooked brown rice

1 cup sugar snap peas

1 cup chopped celery

½ cup dried cranberries

Curry Dressing

In a large nonstick skillet, heat the olive oil over medium heat. Add the mushrooms and sauté until they have softened and most of the liquid has evaporated, about 10 minutes. Transfer to a large bowl and add the chicken, rice, snap peas, celery, cranberries, and dressing. Gently toss until well combined. Cover and refrigerate for at least 30 minutes before serving.

Per serving: 436 calories, 28 g protein, 46 g carbohydrates, 16 g total fat, 3 g saturated fat, 60 mg cholesterol, 5 g dietary fiber, 333 mg sodium

Curry Dressing

Serves 4

1 tablespoon curry powder

1 tablespoon hot water

¼ cup reduced-fat mayonnaise

¼ cup low-fat plain yogurt, preferably Greek

Juice of ½ lemon

1 tablespoon olive oil

½ teaspoon minced garlic

½ teaspoon sugar

Salt and pepper to taste

Place the curry powder in a small bowl, stir in the hot water, and let stand 5 minutes. Add the mayonnaise, yogurt, lemon juice, oil, garlic, sugar, and salt and pepper. Whisk together until well combined.

Cooking Chicken Breasts

One 6-ounce chicken breast gives you approximately 1 cup cubed or shredded cooked chicken. Here are three quick and easy preparations.

Sautéed Chicken Breasts

Sprinkle boneless, skinless chicken breasts with salt, pepper, and dried thyme (optional) to taste. Heat oil in a large nonstick skillet over medium-high heat. Add the chicken and cook 3 minutes per side to brown. Reduce heat to low, add 3 tablespoons water, cover, and cook gently until the chicken is no longer pink in the center but not dry, about 8 minutes longer.

Poached Chicken Breasts

Place chicken breasts in a saucepan and add cold water to cover by 1". Add salt to taste, ¼ teaspoon black peppercorns, 1 bay leaf, ¼ teaspoon dried thyme, 1 chopped scallion, and a few celery leaves if you have some. Bring to a simmer, reduce the heat, and cook at a low simmer until the chicken is no longer pink in the center, about 10 minutes. Remove from the liquid and let cool.

Grilled Chicken Breasts

Preheat a grill or grill pan. Brush chicken breasts with olive oil and sprinkle with salt and pepper. Grill, turning once, until no longer pink in the center but not dry, 8 to 12 minutes.

Mandarin Chicken Salad with Honey-Sesame Dressing

This tasty, crunchy salad provides a wide range of textures and flavors. Serve it as a luncheon dish with some herbed flatbread or sesame crackers.

Serves 4 as an entrée

2 boneless, skinless chicken breasts (¾ pound)

½ cup pineapple juice

One 6-ounce container frozen orange juice concentrate

½ cup reduced-sodium soy sauce

1 teaspoon minced fresh ginger

6 cups salad greens

1 cup seedless red grape halves

2 scallions (white and green parts), chopped

½ cup finely chopped fresh cilantro

½ cup toasted almond slices

One 8.4-ounce can mandarin orange slices, drained

Honey-Sesame Dressing

Place the chicken in a deep baking dish. In a small bowl combine the pineapple juice, orange juice concentrate, soy sauce, and ginger and whisk until blended. Pour the mixture over the chicken and cover. Let marinate in the refrigerator overnight or for a minimum of 5 hours.

Preheat the oven to 350°F. Bake the chicken until no longer pink in the center, 30 minutes. Let cool and shred.

Combine the chicken, greens, grapes, scallions, cilantro, almonds, and oranges in a large bowl. Add the dressing, toss until well combined, and serve.

Per serving: 395 calories, 20 g protein, 35 g carbohydrates, 21 g total fat, 3 g saturated fat, 34 mg cholesterol, 5 g dietary fiber, 600 mg sodium

Honey-Sesame Dressing

Serves 4

3 tablespoons lemon juice

2 tablespoons sesame oil

2 tablespoons vegetable oil

1 tablespoon honey

1 teaspoon dry mustard

In a small bowl, combine all of the ingredients and whisk until combined.

A WORD ABOUT WELLNESS

The skin of red and purple grapes is rich in phytochemicals and flavonoids that promote heart health by neutralizing free radicals, preventing the buildup of plaque in arteries; they also raise levels of nitric acid, which may help to keep blood vessels open and blood flowing throughout the body.

Gorgonzola Chicken Salad with Garlic-Chive Dressing

Packed with protein and flavor, this salad makes for a filling meal. Add a bowl of your favorite vegetable-based soup for a complete dinner.

Serves 4 as an entrée

6 cups spinach, washed thoroughly, stemmed, and torn into bite-size pieces

2 cups cubed cooked chicken breast (see page 75)

Cooked kernels from 1 ear corn (see page 50), or 1 cup frozen corn, thawed in the microwave 1 to 2 minutes

4 ounces Gorgonzola cheese, crumbled

6 strips bacon or turkey bacon, cooked, drained, and crumbled

2 hard-cooked eggs or egg whites, chopped

½ cup pecans, toasted (see page 30)

½ cup shredded carrot

⅓ cup chopped scallions (white and green parts)

Garlic-Chive Dressing

Combine all of the ingredients in a large bowl and gently toss until well combined.

Per serving: 700 calories, 39 g protein, 15 g carbohydrates, 56 g total fat, 14 g saturated fat, 201 mg cholesterol, 5 g dietary fiber, 735 mg sodium

Garlic-Chive Dressing

Serves 4

½ cup olive oil

Juice of 1 lemon

1 large clove garlic, minced

2 teaspoons fresh chives, finely chopped

½ teaspoon dry mustard

In a blender, combine all the ingredients and blend until smooth.

Asian Pasta Salad with Chicken

While this salad calls for a large number of ingredients, it's worth the effort, I promise! The pungent taste of fresh ginger is fantastic. You need only a little of it to go a long way. The flavorful salad also calls for the rich, nutty taste of Asian toasted sesame oil. You can find it in most grocery stores and Asian markets. The salad works well with any pasta shape, so go ahead and use your favorite.

Serves 4 as an entrée

½ pound angel hair or capellini pasta, preferably whole grain

2 cups bean sprouts

2 tablespoons canola oil

3 tablespoons Asian toasted sesame oil

2 cups shredded cooked chicken breast (see page 75)

1 red bell pepper, seeded and cut into thin strips

2 scallions (green and white parts), thinly sliced

1½ teaspoons grated or minced fresh ginger, or 1 teaspoon dry

1½ teaspoons minced garlic

6 tablespoons reduced-sodium soy sauce

1 tablespoon creamy peanut butter

1 tablespoon red wine vinegar

1 teaspoon hot pepper sauce

1 tablespoon chopped roasted peanuts

Cook the pasta in a large pot of boiling, salted water until al dente, about 5 minutes. Add the bean sprouts, wait 10 seconds, then drain the contents of the pot in a colander. Transfer to a large mixing bowl. Add the canola oil and 1 tablespoon of the sesame oil and toss. Add the chicken, red pepper, scallions, ginger, and garlic. Set aside.

In a food processor, blend the soy sauce, peanut butter, vinegar, hot pepper sauce, and remaining 2 tablespoons sesame oil. Pour over the salad and toss. Sprinkle with the peanuts and serve.

Per serving: 564 calories, 34 g protein, 51 g carbohydrates, 25 g total fat, 3 g saturated fat, 60 mg cholesterol, 7 g dietary fiber, 980 mg sodium

Preparing Fresh Ginger

Although fresh ginger may be peeled and chopped, the easiest way to handle it is to leave the skin on and grate it, either with the fine holes of a grater or a microplane.

Mexican Cornbread Salad with Chicken Sausage

Cornbread, jalapeños, and chicken sausage make this salad a real winner. Make it with prepared cornbread or cornbread muffins, but make sure the cornbread is made without a lot of sugar or corn syrup (check the ingredient list—corn syrup should not be the first ingredient!).

Serves 4 as an entrée

2 teaspoons canola oil

1 pound chicken sausage, whatever variety you like, sliced ½" thick

8 cups bite-size pieces chicory or other lettuce

4 cups 1"-cubed cornbread or corn muffins

2 tomatoes, cored and cubed

2 cups chopped green bell pepper

2 cups chopped red bell pepper

Two 11-ounce cans mandarin oranges, drained (about 2 cups)

2 cups sliced fennel or celery

1 cup slivered almonds, toasted (see page 30)

1 jalapeño chile pepper, seeded and chopped (wear plastic gloves when handling)

2 teaspoons finely chopped fresh sage, or ½ teaspoon dried

Orange Dressing

Heat the oil in a large nonstick skillet over medium heat. Add the sausage slices and cook, turning, until lightly browned and cooked through, 7 to 10 minutes.

In a large bowl, combine the sausage, chicory or lettuce, cornbread or muffins, tomatoes, green pepper, red pepper, oranges, fennel or celery, almonds, jalapeño, and sage. Add the dressing, toss gently, and serve.

Per serving: *893 calories, 41 g protein, 67 g carbohydrates, 56 g total fat, 7 g saturated fat, 117 mg cholesterol, 26 g dietary fiber, 1,089 mg sodium*

Orange Dressing with a Kick

Serves 4

½ cup + 2 tablespoons orange juice

7 tablespoons canola oil

2 tablespoons white wine vinegar

1 teaspoon chopped red jalapeño chile pepper (wear plastic gloves when handling)

Salt and pepper to taste

Whisk together all of the ingredients in a small bowl until well combined.

Sweet Potato Slaw with Chicken

I love the taste of raw sweet potato. It is slightly sweet, like a carrot, and wonderful when grated into salads. And it's a quick way to get a boost of beta-carotene into your diet. This recipe calls for broccoli slaw, a combination of prepared shredded broccoli, carrot, and cabbage that is available in the produce aisle of most grocery stores.

Serves 4 as an entrée

1 small sweet potato, peeled and grated on the large holes of a grater

One 16-ounce bag broccoli slaw

1 Granny Smith apple, cored but not peeled, and cut into thin strips

⅓ cup chopped red onion

¼ cup apple juice

Salt and pepper to taste

2 boneless, skinless chicken breasts (¾–1 pound)

½ teaspoon dried thyme

1 tablespoon olive oil

8 cups bite-size pieces mixed romaine and red leaf lettuces

¼ cup dried cranberries

⅓ cup walnut pieces, toasted (see page 30) and chopped

Apple Cider Dressing (page 126), prepared without the sugar

Toss together the sweet potato, broccoli slaw, apple, onion, apple juice, and salt and set aside to marinate while you cook the chicken.

Sprinkle the chicken with the thyme and salt and pepper. Heat the oil in a large nonstick skillet over medium-high heat. Add the chicken and cook 3 minutes per side to brown. Reduce the heat to low, add 3 tablespoons water, cover, and cook gently until the chicken is no longer pink in the center but not dry, about 8 minutes longer. Cut into slices and add to the bowl with the slaw mixture. Add the lettuces, cranberries, walnuts, and dressing, toss to combine, and serve.

Per serving: 497 calories, 25 g protein, 25 g carbohydrates, 32 g total fat, 4 g saturated fat, 49 mg cholesterol, 8 g dietary fiber, 240 mg sodium

Wiley's Wisdom

Walnuts are a good source of omega-3 fatty acids. Researchers believe that omega-3s may improve your memory and uplift your mood. Keep walnuts handy and sprinkle them often on your salads. You can buy them toasted or toast them yourself (see page 30).

Grilled Chicken Salad with Barley and Summer Vegetables

Grilled pineapple and a balsamic vinaigrette give this salad a sweet-and-sour flavor boost. Barley helps add bulk to satisfy hungry appetites.

Serves 4 as an entrée

1½ cups water

Salt

¾ cup quick-cooking barley

2 boneless, skinless chicken breasts (about 1 pound)

Balsamic Vinaigrette (page 107)

One 6-ounce package whole portobello mushroom caps

1 zucchini (about ½ pound), sliced ⅛" thick on an angle

1 yellow squash (about ½ pound), sliced ⅛" thick on an angle

1 red bell pepper, seeded and cut into 1"-wide strips

2 slices (1"-thick) fresh or canned pineapple, drained

1–2 tablespoons oil, for grilling

8 cups arugula

Bring the water to a boil with salt to taste in a saucepan. Add the barley, reduce the heat, and simmer, covered, until tender, about 10 minutes. Remove from heat and let stand, covered, 5 minutes.

Meanwhile, put the chicken in a bowl and pour over 3 tablespoons of the vinaigrette. Put the mushrooms in another bowl, add 5 tablespoons vinaigrette, and toss. Let the chicken and mushrooms marinate at least 10 minutes at room temperature, or up to 2 hours, covered, in the refrigerator.

Prepare a medium-hot grill or grill pan. Brush the zucchini, squash, red pepper, and pineapple lightly with oil. Grill the vegetables and pineapple, turning once, until softened and browned, about 10 minutes. Transfer to a bowl. Grill the mushrooms 5 minutes per side and transfer to the bowl. Grill the chicken, turning once, until no longer pink in the center, 16 to 20 minutes. Let the chicken rest 5 minutes.

Cut the chicken into ¼"-thick slices. Cut the pineapple and mushrooms into chunks. Combine the barley, chicken, pineapple, and grilled vegetables in a bowl. Add the remaining vinaigrette and toss. Line a platter with the arugula, spoon the salad and dressing on top, and serve.

Per serving: 362 calories, 34 g protein, 45 g carbohydrates, 6 g total fat, 1 g saturated fat, 66 mg cholesterol, 10 g dietary fiber, 175 mg sodium

Thai Chicken Salad

This dish is inspired by the chicken salad at one of my favorite Thai restaurants, Siam Square in Great Barrington, Massachusetts. It offers many of the classic Thai flavors including cilantro, lime, and chile pepper. The salad can also be made with napa cabbage.

Serves 4 as an entrée

1 small onion, halved through the root end and thinly sliced (about 1 cup)

White vinegar

4 cups 1"-cubed cooked chicken breast (see page 75)

8 cups bite-size pieces red leaf lettuce

½ large head slivered green cabbage (about 4 cups)

½ small head slivered red cabbage (about 2 cups)

2 large carrots, finely shredded on a box grater

¼ cup toasted sesame seeds (see page 130)

Thai Dressing

½ cup chopped fresh mint, or 1 tablespoon dried (optional)

½ cup chopped fresh cilantro, or 1 tablespoon dried (optional)

Put the onion in a small bowl and add just enough vinegar to cover. Let sit 15 minutes; drain, rinse under cold water, and squeeze out excess vinegar.

In a large bowl, combine the onion, chicken, lettuce, green cabbage, red cabbage, carrots, sesame seeds, and dressing. Toss the salad to combine and sprinkle with fresh mint and cilantro if using.

Per serving: 545 calories, 49 g protein, 22 g carbohydrates, 28 g total fat, 3 g saturated fat, 119 mg cholesterol, 5 g dietary fiber, 642 mg sodium

Thai Dressing

Serves 4

⅓ cup canola oil

3 tablespoons fresh lime juice

3 tablespoons reduced-sodium soy sauce

1 tablespoon brown sugar

1 large clove garlic, minced

1–2 teaspoons seeded and chopped fresh red chile pepper (wear plastic gloves when handling)

Salt and pepper to taste

Whisk all of the ingredients together in a bowl until well combined.

Chicken Pasta Salad with Tomatoes, Spinach, and Broccoli

Most pasta salads come with a thick covering of mayonnaise. Not only is it unhealthy, but it also proves to be a real problem if you plan on bringing a salad to a picnic where it may sit out for a few hours. You won't have that problem here. This version is much cleaner and healthier, as it uses olive oil. For the best flavor, serve the salad warm or at room temperature. To dress it up, try using shrimp, scallops, or even sliced beef instead of chicken.

Serves 4 as an entrée

4 tablespoons olive oil

2 cloves garlic, thinly sliced

8 basil leaves, torn into small pieces

2 tomatoes, cored, seeded, and cut into ½" cubes (about 3 cups)

¼ cup chopped red onion

½ pound penne or other pasta, preferably whole grain

1 large head broccoli, cut into florets

1 cup frozen green peas

2 cups shredded cooked chicken breast (see page 75)

4 cups bite-size pieces spinach

Salt and pepper to taste

Combine 3 tablespoons of the oil, the garlic, and basil in a large bowl. Add the tomatoes and onion and stir. Set aside to marinate.

Bring a large pot of salted water to a boil. Add the penne and cook for the number of minutes suggested on the package, but 3 minutes before the pasta is cooked, add the broccoli. A minute later, add the peas. When the pasta is done, drain the pasta and vegetables in a colander.

Add the pasta and vegetables to the bowl with the tomatoes. Add the chicken and spinach and season with salt and pepper. Toss gently. Transfer to a serving bowl, drizzle with the remaining 1 tablespoon oil, and serve.

Per serving: 548 calories, 37 g protein, 63 g carbohydrates, 18 g total fat, 3 g saturated fat, 60 mg cholesterol, 9 g dietary fiber, 246 mg sodium

Spinach is one of those vegetables that we all know is loaded with beneficial vitamins, minerals, and other nutrients. Lutein is one of them. Studies indicate that lutein-rich foods—like salad made with baby spinach—may, in fact, reduce the risks of developing colon cancer. Lutein, along with zeaxanthin, are pigments in the eyes that seem to be able to "disarm" free radicals before they can do damage, such as cause cataracts and macular degeneration, a leading cause of blindness in the elderly.

Spinach is definitely a "powerhouse" food, so be sure to add an extra cup of spinach to your next salad.

Chicken and Wild Rice Salad with Butternut Squash and Dried Cherries

To speed up preparation of this salad, look for prepared (peeled and cubed) butternut squash in your produce department, but use it soon after purchase—it will only last a couple of days in the refrigerator. If you like, you may also finish this salad with ½ cup grated Cheddar or Jack cheese, or crumbled goat cheese, blue cheese, or feta cheese.

Serves 4 as an entrée

¾ cup wild rice or wild rice blend

1½ cups water

Salt to taste

1 head broccoli, cut into florets

2 tablespoons canola oil

1 pound butternut squash, peeled and cut into ½" cubes

Pepper to taste

6 to 8 cups arugula

2 cups cubed cooked chicken breast (see page 75)

½ cup dried cherries or cranberries

Shallot–Red Wine Vinaigrette (page 137)

Combine the rice, water, and salt in a saucepan. Bring to a boil and reduce the heat to very low. Cover and simmer until the rice is tender and all the water has been absorbed, 40 to 45 minutes (or as noted on package). Let stand, covered and off the heat, for 10 minutes.

Bring a saucepan of salted water to a boil. Add the broccoli and cook until just tender, 2 to 3 minutes. Drain and rinse under cold running water to stop the cooking. Transfer to a bowl.

Heat the oil in a large skillet over medium heat. Add the squash, sprinkle with salt and pepper, and cook, turning the pieces as needed for even color, until cooked through and golden brown, 5 to 7 minutes. Let cool a few minutes, then add to the bowl with the broccoli. Add the cooked rice, arugula, chicken, cherries or cranberries, and dressing. Toss gently and serve.

Per serving: 599 calories, 33 g protein, 60 g carbohydrates, 28 g total fat, 4 g saturated fat, 60 mg cholesterol, 13 g dietary fiber, 263 mg sodium

Southwestern Chicken Salad with Cumin-Lime Vinaigrette

The chili powder and cumin spice in the dressing really bring out the fruit and vegetable flavors in this authentic Tex-Mex salad.

Serves 4 as an entrée

1 pound shredded red or green cabbage (about 9 cups) or coleslaw mix

2 cups cubed grilled chicken breast (see page 75)

1 red or green bell pepper, seeded and cut into thin strips

Cooked kernels from 2 ears corn (see page 50), or 2 cups frozen corn, thawed in the microwave 1 to 2 minutes

1 tomato, sliced, slices cut into strips, or 1 cup halved cherry tomatoes

⅓ pound snow peas, cut into long, thin strips

2 slices (½"-thick) fresh or canned pineapple, cut into chunks

2 scallions (white and green parts), chopped

⅔ cup chopped fresh cilantro, or 1 tablespoon dried

Cumin-Lime Vinaigrette

1 avocado, halved, pitted, peeled, and cut into chunks

In a large bowl, combine the cabbage, chicken, bell pepper, corn, tomato, snow peas, pineapple, scallions, and cilantro. Add the dressing and toss. Let stand 15 minutes to allow the cabbage to absorb the dressing. Just before serving, fold in the avocado.

Per serving: 588 calories, 27 g protein, 70 g carbohydrates, 23 g total fat, 4 g saturated fat, 60 mg cholesterol, 10 g dietary fiber, 170 mg sodium

Cumin-Lime Vinaigrette

Serves 4

¼ cup olive oil

¼ cup fresh lime juice

1 tablespoon white wine vinegar

1 teaspoon ground cumin

½ teaspoon chili powder

Salt and pepper to taste

Whisk together all of the ingredients in a small bowl until well combined.

Chicken Salad with Broccoli Rabe and Plums

The combination of fresh plums, broccoli rabe, and chicken makes this elegant salad far from typical. Broccoli rabe is in the same vegetable family as regular broccoli, but has a more distinctive, bitter taste and a leafier appearance. It is often used in Southern Italian cooking. Try making this delicious sweet and savory salad with a large pear when plums are out of season.

Serves 4 as an entrée

1 bunch broccoli rabe

4 tablespoons olive oil

2 cloves garlic, chopped

Salt

¼ teaspoon red pepper flakes

1 red bell pepper, seeded and diced

¼ cup chopped red onion

8 cups baby spinach

3 ripe plums, pitted and sliced

¼ cup fresh lemon juice

¼ teaspoon black pepper

2 chicken breasts (¾ pound), cooked (see page 75) and sliced

¼ cup pine nuts or chopped pecans, toasted (see page 30)

Trim the ends from the broccoli rabe. Cut the bunch crosswise into thirds. Transfer to a bowl, add water to cover, and swish in the water to rinse. Lift out of the bowl and drain in a colander.

Combine 2 tablespoons of the oil and the garlic in a large sauté pan. Place over medium-low heat and cook until the garlic sizzles and just begins to brown. Add the broccoli rabe in 2 batches, stirring the first batch to wilt it (so that the entire bunch will fit into the pan) before adding the rest. Sprinkle with salt to taste and the red pepper flakes, cover, and cook 3 minutes.

Add the bell pepper and onion and cook until the broccoli rabe is tender when you squeeze it between 2 fingers, about 5 minutes. Uncover and cook until all of the water evaporates.

Transfer the vegetables to a large bowl. Add the spinach, plums, lemon juice, remaining 2 tablespoons oil, ¼ teaspoon salt, and ¼ teaspoon black pepper and toss. Divide the salad among 4 plates or shallow bowls. Arrange the sliced chicken on top, scatter the pine nuts or pecans over, and serve.

Per serving: 355 calories, 27 g protein, 15 g carbohydrates, 22 g total fat, 3 g saturated fat, 60 mg cholesterol, 4 g dietary fiber, 223 mg sodium

A WORD ABOUT WELLNESS

Despite its name, broccoli rabe—a slightly bitter-tasting dark green leafy vegetable—isn't a kind of broccoli, although it is in the same botanical family and shares many of broccoli's healthy attributes. Broccoli rabe is rich in cancer-protecting phytochemicals, such as flavonoids, sulforaphane, and indoles, which act to prevent cellular degeneration by helping the liver detoxify chemicals that can act as carcinogens. It is also abundant in vitamins A and C, folate, calcium, and potassium. Both the shoots, which resemble broccoli florets, and the leaves are edible, raw or cooked—and about 30 calories per ½-cup serving.

Chicken Couscous Salad

I like to serve this salad for dinner in the summertime when I entertain friends out on my back deck. The dish is filled with the clean, bright, distinctive taste of mint and cilantro. Be sure to chop the herbs on the larger side so you get a good amount of flavor with every bite. Couscous, a fast-cooking pasta with grainlike texture, can be found in the rice aisle of most grocery stores.

Serves 4 as an entrée

1 cup orange juice

1 cup water

Salt to taste

One 9-ounce package couscous

3 cups shredded cooked chicken breast (see page 75)

2 cups grated (on the large holes of a grater) carrot (about 2 large)

2 cups halved seedless red or green grapes

1 cup frozen green peas, thawed

1 cup sliced celery

3 scallions (white and green parts), sliced

¼ cup sliced green olives

¼ cup sliced almonds

2 tablespoons roughly chopped fresh mint

2 tablespoons roughly chopped fresh cilantro

Bright Lemon Dressing (page 65)

Pepper to taste

12 cups bite-size pieces romaine lettuce

Combine the orange juice, water, and salt in a saucepan or microwaveable glass container and bring to a boil over medium-high heat; or cover and microwave until boiling. Remove from the heat, stir in the couscous, cover, and let stand until the couscous has absorbed all of the liquid, about 5 minutes. Fluff with a fork.

In a large bowl, combine the couscous, chicken, carrot, grapes, peas, celery, scallions, olives, almonds, mint, and cilantro. Add the dressing, season with pepper, and stir.

Make a bed of lettuce on each of 4 plates, spoon the salad on top, and serve.

Per serving: 730 calories, 48 g protein, 87 g carbohydrates, 22 g total fat, 3 g saturated fat, 90 mg cholesterol, 11 g dietary fiber, 354 mg sodium

Mexican Chicken Salad

This flavorful salad offers all of the taste of a delicious Mexican meal, without all of the fat and calories.

4 cups ¾"-cubed cooked chicken breast (see page 75)

1 pint cherry tomatoes, halved, or quartered if large

Cooked kernels from 4 ears corn (see page 50), or 4 cups frozen corn, thawed in the microwave 1 to 2 minutes

1 green bell pepper, seeded and diced

1 cup halved seedless red or green grapes

¼ cup chopped red onion

½ cup loosely packed fresh cilantro leaves (including slender stems), roughly chopped

Jalapeño-Lime Vinaigrette

1 avocado, halved, pitted, peeled, and cut into bite-size chunks

4 cups mixed greens

In a large bowl, combine the chicken, tomatoes, corn, green pepper, grapes, onion, cilantro, and vinaigrette and toss. Gently fold in the avocado.

Divide the mixed greens among 4 plates. Top with the chicken salad and serve.

Per serving: 637 calories, 50 g protein, 45 g carbohydrates, 31 g total fat, 5 g saturated fat, 119 mg cholesterol, 9 g dietary fiber, 205 mg sodium

Jalapeño-Lime Vinaigrette

⅓ cup olive oil

¼ cup fresh lime juice (from about 2 limes)

2 jalapeño chile peppers, seeded and finely chopped (wear plastic gloves when handling)

Salt and pepper to taste

Whisk together all of the ingredients in a small bowl until well combined.

Wiley's Wisdom

Some people think that mesclun is a type of lettuce. Actually, mesclun is the name give to a mixture of tender salad leaves. Originally created in France, it has become popular all over the world. It usually includes radicchio, arugula, dandelion greens, romaine lettuce, and endive. Parsley and basil may also be included.

Chicory Salad with Chicken and Raspberry-Pomegranate Dressing

Chicory, escarole, and endive are all greens whose bitter flavor goes well with fruit, sweet potatoes, and a sweet dressing such as this one.

Serves 4 as an entrée

1 sweet potato, peeled, quartered lengthwise, and sliced ½" thick

½ pound Brussels sprouts, bottoms trimmed, large sprouts cut in half

2 tablespoons olive oil

Salt and pepper to taste

8 cups bite-size pieces bitter greens, such as chicory, escarole, or endive

2 cups cubed cooked chicken breast (see page 75)

1 cup chopped celery and leaves

1 cup seedless green grapes, halved

16 pimiento-stuffed green olives

¼ cup chopped fresh parsley, or 1 tablespoon dried

Raspberry-Pomegranate Vinaigrette (page 34)

1 cup pomegranate seeds

Preheat the oven to 425°F. Place the sweet potato and Brussels sprouts on a baking sheet. Drizzle with the oil, sprinkle with salt and pepper, and toss. Roast until the vegetables are lightly browned on one side, about 15 minutes. Turn the pieces, and roast until the vegetables are cooked through, 10 to 15 minutes longer. Let cool 5 minutes, then transfer to a large bowl.

Add the greens, chicken, celery, grapes, olives, parsley, and dressing and toss. Sprinkle the pomegranate seeds on top and serve.

Per serving: *540 calories, 31 g protein, 49 g carbohydrates, 27 g total fat, 4 g saturated fat, 60 mg cholesterol, 19 g dietary fiber, 733 mg sodium*

Wiley's Wisdom

If you need to prepare a salad hours in advance of serving, wash the greens and run them through a salad spinner. Wrap them in dye-free paper towels, place in a large bowl, and refrigerate. The paper towels will soak up the remaining water and your greens will be crisp and dry for your salad when you're ready to serve.

Pita Chicken Salad

Delicious on its own, served over a bed of romaine lettuce, or as a filling for a whole wheat pita pocket, this salad's bright flavors come from the combination of lemony mayonnaise and crisp, tart apples.

Serves 4 as an entrée

4 cups cubed cooked chicken breast (see page 75)

1 sharp apple, such as Granny Smith or Braeburn, cored and cut into bite-size pieces

¾ cup chopped celery (about 3 small ribs)

1 green bell pepper, seeded and diced

2 scallions (white and green parts), thinly sliced

8 basil leaves, torn into pieces, or ½ teaspoon dried basil

Lemon Mayonnaise

⅓ cup toasted pecans (see page 30), chopped

8 cups bite-size pieces romaine lettuce

4 whole wheat pitas

Combine the chicken, apple, celery, bell pepper, scallions, basil, and mayonnaise in a large bowl and toss to coat all of the ingredients with the mayonnaise. Fold in the pecans. Divide the lettuce among 4 plates and top with the chicken salad. Serve the pitas alongside.

Per serving: 723 calories, 53 g protein, 57 g carbohydrates, 34 g total fat, 2 g saturated fat, 139 mg cholesterol, 10 g dietary fiber, 1,140 mg sodium

Lemon Mayonnaise

Serves 4

1 cup reduced-fat mayonnaise

¼ cup fresh lemon juice (from about 2 lemons)

1 tablespoon Dijon mustard

⅛ teaspoon cayenne pepper

Salt and pepper to taste

Whisk together all of the ingredients in a small bowl until well combined.

Hail Caesar Salad

Back at the University of Alabama, one of my English literature professors always entered the classroom and declared, "Hail, Caesar!" I am reminded of him whenever I eat this salad. Unlike the typical overdressed Caesar salads you find on most restaurant tables, this version uses a whole lot less fat and a whole lot more vegetables. Use store-bought croutons or make your own with the recipe on the opposite page.

Serves 4 as an entrée

2 cloves garlic, crushed with the side of a large knife and peeled

2 anchovy fillets, chopped

2 teaspoons Worcestershire sauce

½ teaspoon dry mustard

1 rounded tablespoon reduced-fat mayonnaise

⅓ cup olive oil

Juice of ½ lemon (about 1 tablespoon)

8 cups bite-size pieces romaine lettuce

1½ cups sliced mushrooms

1 cup halved cherry tomatoes

2 boneless, skinless chicken breast halves (about ½ pound), cooked (see page 75) and sliced

½ cup grated Parmesan cheese

Pepper to taste

2 cups Homemade Croutons

In a large bowl, mash together the garlic and anchovies with a fork until the mixture almost forms a paste. Mix in the Worcestershire sauce and mustard, then the mayonnaise. Slowly whisk in the olive oil, and then the lemon juice.

Add the lettuce, mushrooms, tomatoes, and chicken to the dressing and toss. Add the cheese and a liberal amount of pepper. Add the croutons, toss well to combine, and serve.

Per serving: 661 calories, 31 g protein, 51 g carbohydrates, 38 g total fat, 7 g saturated fat, 61 mg cholesterol, 7 g dietary fiber, 1,438 mg sodium

Homemade Croutons

Serves 4

2 tablespoons olive oil

1 baguette, thinly sliced

Preheat the oven to 400°F. Spread the oil on a baking sheet. Press each baguette slice into the oil, then turn, so that both sides are coated with the oil. Bake, turning the slices once about halfway through the cooking, until golden brown, 8 to 10 minutes.

Grilled Sweet Potato and Turkey Salad with Honey-Mustard Vinaigrette

This recipe is the perfect reason to break out the grill in the fall or winter! You can, however, use a grill pan or broiler as well. Try grilling extra-firm tofu (see page 129) as an alternative to ground turkey.

Serves 4 as an entrée

2 sweet potatoes, peeled and sliced into ½" rounds

3 tablespoons olive oil

Four 4-ounce ground turkey patties

4 cups spinach

1 cup diced yellow bell pepper

4 scallions (white and green parts), chopped

2 slices bacon or turkey bacon, cooked and crumbled

Honey-Mustard Vinaigrette

Prepare a hot grill or grill pan. Brush the sweet potatoes with the oil and place on the grill. Grill, turning once, until tender, about 10 minutes. (Alternately, arrange the sweet potato slices in a single layer on a large baking sheet and brush with the oil. Broil on high until the edges turn light brown, 8 to 10 minutes.)

While the sweet potatoes are cooking, add the turkey patties to the grill and cook, turning once, until a thermometer inserted in the centers reaches 165°F, about 8 minutes. (Alternately, place the patties on a baking sheet and broil on high for 3 minutes. Turn the patties over and broil for another 2 minutes.)

Let the sweet potatoes and turkey patties cool slightly, then cut into 1" cubes and place in a large bowl. Add the spinach, yellow pepper, scallions, bacon, and vinaigrette and gently toss until well combined.

Per serving: 472 calories, 32 g protein, 20 g carbohydrates, 31 g total fat, 4 g saturated fat, 49 mg cholesterol, 4 g dietary fiber, 306 mg sodium

Honey-Mustard Vinaigrette

Serves 4

⅓ cup olive oil

3 tablespoons white wine vinegar

1 tablespoon prepared honey mustard

1 clove garlic, minced

Salt and pepper to taste

Whisk together all of the ingredients in a small bowl until well combined. Let stand for 5 minutes before using.

Turkey and Wild Rice Salad

The perfect use for leftover wild rice or turkey, this salad can easily be doubled or tripled for a post-Thanksgiving crowd. Feel free to substitute chicken or tofu for the turkey.

Serves 4 as an entrée

3 cups cooked wild rice

2 cups cubed cooked turkey

1 cup cooked asparagus cut into 1" pieces

½ cup cooked peas

½ cup golden raisins

½ cup pecan halves, toasted (see page 30)

½ small red onion, finely diced

Red Wine–Maple Vinaigrette

Combine all of the ingredients in a large salad bowl and gently toss until well combined. Cover and refrigerate for up to 3 hours before serving.

Per serving: 594 calories, 30 g protein, 52 g carbohydrates, 31 g total fat, 4 g saturated fat, 48 mg cholesterol, 7 g dietary fiber, 143 mg sodium

Red Wine–Maple Vinaigrette

Serves 4

⅓ cup olive oil

3 tablespoons red wine vinegar

1 tablespoon maple syrup

1 teaspoon prepared mustard

Salt and pepper to taste

Whisk together all of the ingredients in a small bowl until well combined.

Turkey Salad with Baked Potatoes and Broccoli

This salad is a great way to enjoy potatoes without all of the fat that can accompany many familiar side dishes, such as mashed potatoes or potato gratin. The potatoes here can be served hot out of the oven, or at room temperature. In winter use cherry tomatoes instead of regular tomatoes, as they provide a sweet flavor year-round.

Serves 4 as an entrée

4 baking potatoes

1 head broccoli, trimmed and cut into florets

8 cups arugula

1½ pounds tomatoes, cut into 1" dice

Cooked kernels from 1 ear corn (see page 50), or 1 cup frozen corn, thawed in the microwave 1 to 2 minutes

¼ cup chopped fresh parsley

2 teaspoons drained capers (optional)

2 teaspoons balsamic vinegar

2 teaspoons olive oil

Salt and pepper to taste

Horseradish Dressing (page 111)

1 cup shredded Cheddar cheese

2 scallions (white and green parts), thinly sliced

¾ pound sliced deli turkey

Preheat the oven to 400°F. Use a fork to poke a few holes in each potato to keep them from bursting during baking. Roast until tender when pierced with a sharp knife, about 1 hour.

Bring about 1" water to a boil in the bottom of a steamer or saucepan. Put the broccoli florets in the steamer basket, place over the boiling water, cover, and steam until just tender, 5 to 6 minutes. Drain in a colander, cool under cold running water, and drain again.

Transfer the broccoli to a large bowl, and add the arugula, tomatoes, corn, parsley, capers if using, vinegar, oil, and salt and pepper. Toss until well combined. Divide among 4 large plates.

Cut each potato almost in half, leaving the skin attached on the bottom to hold its shape, and use a fork to loosen the potato from the skin. Season with salt and pepper. Add a couple of big spoonfuls of dressing to each potato and stir with the fork. Place each stuffed potato on top of a salad and sprinkle with the cheese and scallions. Arrange the turkey slices around the potatoes and serve.

Per serving: 466 calories, 33 g protein, 35 g carbohydrates, 25 g total fat, 9 g saturated fat, 73 mg cholesterol, 12 g dietary fiber, 1,436 mg sodium

New Orleans Dirty Rice Salad

This salad is inspired by the traditional New Orleans side dish of dirty rice. It's usually made with ground chicken livers—in this healthier salad version, ground turkey makes a fitting substitute.

Serves 4 as an entrée

¾ cup brown rice

1¾ cups water

Salt and pepper

One 10-ounce package frozen okra or 1 pound fresh okra, trimmed and sliced

3 tablespoons canola oil

1 cup chopped onion

1 green bell pepper, seeded and chopped

2 cloves garlic, chopped

½ pound ground turkey breast

One 15.5-ounce can red beans, drained and rinsed

2 tomatoes, chopped

¼ cup chopped fresh parsley, or 1 tablespoon dried

6 cups spinach, arugula, or romaine lettuce

Hot Pepper Dressing (page 49)

Combine the rice, water, and salt to taste in a small saucepan. Bring to a boil over high heat. Reduce the heat, cover, and simmer until tender, 40 to 45 minutes. Let stand, covered, 10 minutes. Transfer to a large mixing bowl and cool to room temperature.

Meanwhile, in a small saucepan, cook the okra in boiling salted water, 1 to 2 minutes for frozen or 5 minutes for fresh. Drain and transfer to a separate bowl.

Heat 2 tablespoons of the oil in a large skillet over medium heat. Add the onion and cook 1 minute. Add the green pepper and cook, stirring, until tender, about 7 minutes. Add the garlic and cook 1 minute. Season to taste with salt and pepper and add to the bowl with the okra.

Heat the remaining 1 tablespoon oil in the skillet over high heat. Add the turkey and cook, stirring, until it loses its pink color, about 5 minutes. Season with salt and pepper to taste. Return the cooked vegetables to the skillet along with the beans and stir to combine. Let cool to room temperature.

In a serving bowl, combine the rice, turkey-vegetable mixture, tomatoes, parsley, greens, and dressing. Toss well and serve.

Per serving: 607 calories, 26 g protein, 61 g carbohydrates, 31 g total fat, 4 g saturated fat, 23 mg cholesterol, 13 g dietary fiber, 249 mg sodium

Wiley's Wisdom

The leanest poultry comes from skinless breast of chicken and turkey. Skinless dark meat has almost twice the fat calories of the breast. If you're trying to cut the fat and you like ground chicken or ground turkey, select only the packages that say they are made from skinless ground breast meat.

Turkey-Potato Salad with Green Olive Vinaigrette

The potatoes in this salad sop up the rich, sharp taste of the green olives in the vinaigrette. The smoked turkey also plays nicely off the flavorful dressing. Buy a thick slice of smoked turkey at the deli counter and cut it into cubes or slices for this salad.

Serves 4 as an entrée

½ pound new potatoes

2 teaspoons white wine vinegar

Salt

2 cups cubed smoked white meat turkey

1 cucumber, peeled and sliced

1 red or green bell pepper, seeded and diced

1 cup halved grape tomatoes

1 cup halved seedless red grapes

½ cup chopped celery

½ cup chopped red onion

½ cup chopped fresh parsley, or 2 tablespoons dried

Black pepper

Green Olive Vinaigrette

8 cups baby spinach or arugula

Cover the potatoes with cold salted water in a saucepan. Bring to a boil, reduce the heat, and simmer until tender when pierced with a small knife, 15 to 25 minutes, depending on size. Let stand until cool enough to handle, then peel and cut into slices. Transfer the warm slices to a bowl, sprinkling each layer with vinegar and salt to taste. Let cool.

Add the turkey, cucumber, bell pepper, tomatoes, grapes, celery, onion, parsley, salt and pepper to taste, and vinaigrette to the potatoes and toss gently. Add the spinach or arugula, toss, and serve. Or serve the potato mixture on top of the greens.

Per serving: 342 calories, 16 g protein, 22 g carbohydrates, 21 g total fat, 3 g saturated fat, 0 mg cholesterol, 6 g dietary fiber, 955 mg sodium

Green Olive Vinaigrette

Serves 4

⅓ cup olive oil

12 green olives, pitted and chopped

2 tablespoons fresh lemon juice

2 tablespoons white wine vinegar

2 teaspoons Dijon mustard

Salt and pepper to taste

Whisk together all of the ingredients in a small bowl until well combined.

Green Bean and Roast Beef Salad with Balsamic-Mustard Vinaigrette

Green beans lend a welcome crunch to this unique salad. The sweet, sharp taste of balsamic vinegar really brings out the natural sugar of the nectarine.

Serves 4 as an entrée

1 pound green beans, trimmed

8 cups watercress, arugula, or bite-size pieces romaine lettuce

2 cups cubed roast beef (from a thick slice of deli roast beef)

1 nectarine, pitted and cut into thin wedges

1 tomato, cored and cut into thin wedges

1 cucumber, peeled and cut into chunks

16 green olives, pitted and cut in half

¼ cup torn fresh basil leaves, or 1 teaspoon dried basil

Balsamic-Mustard Vinaigrette

Bring a saucepan of salted water to a boil. Add the green beans and cook until just tender and still bright green, about 3 minutes. Drain in a colander and rinse under cold running water to stop the cooking. Drain.

Transfer the beans to a large bowl. Add the greens, beef, nectarine, tomato, cucumber, olives, basil, and vinaigrette, and toss. Divide among 4 bowls and serve.

Per serving: 353 calories, 16 g protein, 20 g carbohydrates, 25 g total fat, 4 g saturated fat, 25 mg cholesterol, 5 g dietary fiber, 950 mg sodium

Balsamic-Mustard Vinaigrette

Serves 4

6 tablespoons olive oil

2 tablespoons balsamic vinegar

1½ teaspoons Dijon mustard

Salt and pepper to taste

Whisk together all the ingredients in a small bowl until well combined.

Steak Salad with Soy-Ginger Dressing

A flank steak usually weighs at least 1½ pounds, so you'll probably need to buy more steak than you'll need for this recipe. I recommend cooking the whole thing and using the leftover steak in another recipe, such as Thai Beef Salad with Soy-Lime Dressing (page 108), or Steak and Tomato Salad with Horseradish Dressing (page 110).

Serves 4 as an entrée

½ cup reduced-sodium soy sauce

1 tablespoon grated fresh ginger, or ½ teaspoon dried ginger

2 cloves garlic, crushed with the flat side of a large knife

¾ pound (1"-thick) flank steak

1 cup sugar snap or snow peas

8 cups bite-size pieces romaine lettuce

1 red bell pepper, seeded and cut into thin strips

1 cup sliced radishes

4 cups bean sprouts

Combine the soy sauce, ginger, and garlic in a baking dish. Add the steak, turning to coat, and marinate for 6 hours, or preferably overnight, in the refrigerator.

Prepare a hot grill or preheat the broiler. Remove the steak from the marinade, reserving the marinade. Grill or broil the steak, turning once, until a thermometer inserted in the center reaches 145°F for medium-rare, about 8 minutes. Cut the steak in half lengthwise and then cut each half against the grain into thin slices.

Pour the marinade into a small saucepan and boil 2 minutes. Set aside to cool.

Bring a large saucepan of water to a boil. Add the sugar snap or snow peas and simmer until just tender, about 2 minutes. Drain in a colander.

Combine the lettuce, red pepper, and radishes on a platter. Arrange the snow peas, bean sprouts, and sliced steak on top. Pour the reduced marinade over the salad and serve.

Per serving: 255 calories, 27 g protein, 20 g carbohydrates, 8 g total fat, 3 g saturated fat, 35 mg cholesterol, 7 g dietary fiber, 1,320 mg sodium

A WORD ABOUT WELLNESS

Think twice before you peel fruits and vegetables with edible skins. Because skin is a food's first line of defense against environmental hazards, it harbors more antioxidant benefits than the flesh inside. For example, sugar snap peas and other edible pods such as snow peas supply three times as much vitamin C as shelled peas. Quercetin, a powerful anti-inflammatory antioxidant, is found only in apple skins. The brownish skins on almonds and peanuts contain high concentrations of a polyphenol called ellagic acid that aids in preventing cancer. Scrubbing rather than peeling a potato protects more of its fiber, niacin, iron, and vitamin C. Last but not least, it's generally true that the greater proportion of skin to flesh, the higher the antioxidant values. That is, a cherry tomato has a higher antioxidant content than a beefsteak tomato.

Taco Salad with Fresh Tomato Salsa

Filled with all of the traditional south of the border flavors, minus the extra fat, this salad will satisfy any Mexican food craving you might have. Try doubling or tripling the recipe to feed a crowd.

Serves 4 as an entrée

1 tablespoon canola oil

½ pound lean ground beef or ground turkey breast

½ teaspoon ground cumin

¼ teaspoon ground chili powder

Salt and pepper to taste

8 cups chopped iceberg lettuce

1 avocado, halved, pitted, peeled, and diced

½ large red or green bell pepper, seeded and diced

1 small onion, diced

Cooked kernels from 1 ear corn (see page 50), or ¾ cup frozen corn, thawed in the microwave 1 to 2 minutes

Fresh Tomato Salsa

½ cup (2 ounces) shredded Monterey Jack cheese

½ cup crushed, store-bought baked tortilla chips

Heat the oil in a nonstick skillet over medium-high heat. Add the beef and sprinkle with the cumin, chili powder, and salt and pepper. Cook, stirring occasionally, until the beef is fragrant and no longer pink, about 5 minutes. Remove from the heat and let cool.

Transfer the beef, with any accumulated juices, to a large bowl and add the lettuce, avocado, bell pepper, onion, corn, and salsa. Toss gently until everything is well combined. Divide the salad among 4 plates, top with the cheese and chips, and serve.

Per serving: 363 calories, 19 g protein, 29 g carbohydrates, 21 g total fat, 5 g saturated fat, 43 mg cholesterol, 7 g dietary fiber, 335 mg sodium

Fresh Tomato Salsa

Serves 4

1 large tomato, cored and diced (about 2 cups)

¼ cup chopped fresh cilantro, or 2 teaspoons dried

1 large jalapeño chile pepper, chopped (wear plastic gloves when handling)

1 scallion (white and green parts), thinly sliced

2 cloves garlic, chopped

1 tablespoon cider or white vinegar

Salt to taste

Mix all the ingredients together in a small bowl. Let the mixture sit for at least 30 minutes at room temperature before serving, or up to 5 days in the refrigerator.

A WORD ABOUT WELLNESS

Besides tasting terrific in salads and Mexican dips such as salsa and guacamole, tomatoes and avocados together deliver a one-two punch of lycopene and healthy unsaturated fat. Studies have shown that the fat in avocado helps the body absorb seven times more lycopene, a heart-healthy and cancer-fighting antioxidant that tomatoes have in abundance. Tossing tomatoes with a little extra virgin olive oil, or adding a handful of nuts to a tomato salad, will have the same beneficial effect.

Grilled Steak and Mushroom Salad

This dish will satisfy the hardiest of appetites. It is a wonderful grilled salad for summer and can also be made under the broiler or in a grill pan during colder months.

Serves 4 as an entrée

Balsamic Vinaigrette

½ pound 1"-thick flank steak

One 6-ounce package portobello mushroom caps (4 medium)

8 cups arugula or mixed greens

½ cup sliced red onion

1 pint cherry tomatoes

One 1-ounce piece Parmesan cheese, cut into paper-thin slices with a vegetable peeler

Pour one-third of the vinaigrette over the steak in a shallow dish and turn to coat evenly. Set aside at room temperature for at least 10 minutes while you prepare a medium-hot grill, grill pan, or broiler. Pour half of the remaining vinaigrette over the mushrooms and turn to coat evenly. Marinate for 10 minutes.

Remove the steak and mushrooms from the marinade and discard the marinade. Grill or broil the steak and mushrooms, turning once, until a thermometer inserted in the center of the steak reaches 145°F for medium-rare and the mushrooms are perfectly cooked, about 10 minutes. (If using a broiler, be sure to check the mushrooms each minute, as they may cook faster.) Transfer to a rimmed plate and let rest for 5 minutes. Cut the beef against the grain into ½"-thick slices and the mushrooms into ½"-thick slices.

Toss the greens and onion with the remaining dressing in a bowl. Divide among 4 plates and top with the tomatoes, cheese, steak, and mushrooms. Drizzle any accumulated meat and mushroom juices on top and serve.

Per serving: 413 calories, 18 g protein, 10 g carbohydrates, 34 g total fat, 7 g saturated fat, 29 mg cholesterol, 3 g dietary fiber, 197 mg sodium

Balsamic Vinaigrette

Serves 4

1 cup olive oil

¼ cup balsamic vinegar

2 cloves garlic, minced

2 tablespoons minced fresh rosemary,
or 1 tablespoon dried

1 tablespoon minced fresh thyme, or
1½ teaspoons dried

Salt and pepper to taste

Whisk together all of the ingredients in a small bowl until well combined.

A WORD ABOUT WELLNESS

Known for years by herbalists for its medicinal qualities, rosemary, and particularly its oils, is rich in rosmarinic acid, an anti-inflammatory that could modify inflammatory responses to concentrations of molecules that provoke conditions such as asthma, rheumatoid arthritis, liver disease, and heart disease. Rosemary also is a very good source of antioxidants such as vitamin E and flavonoids. Historically used to try to stimulate and improve memory, rosemary is now shown to contain compounds that protect neurotransmitters necessary for concentration, memory, and healthy brain function.

Thai Beef Salad with Soy-Lime Dressing

This salad offers a range of fresh, intense flavors. You can control the level of heat by increasing or decreasing the amount of chile peppers in the dressing.

Serves 4 as an entrée

½ cup chopped fresh cilantro, plus more for garnish

⅓ cup olive oil

2 tablespoons lime juice or rice wine vinegar

2 tablespoons reduced-sodium soy sauce

2 teaspoons brown sugar

1 large clove garlic, minced

2 teaspoons seeded and chopped red chile peppers (wear plastic gloves when handling)

½ teaspoon black pepper

1 pound cooked sirloin steak, cut into bite-size strips

6 cups butter lettuce

1 cup cherry tomatoes, halved

4 scallions (white and green parts), chopped

1 cucumber, halved, seeded, and thinly sliced

In a blender, combine the cilantro, oil, lime juice or vinegar, soy sauce, brown sugar, garlic, chiles, and black pepper and blend until smooth. Place the steak strips in a deep dish and pour ⅓ cup of the dressing over. Set the remaining dressing aside. Cover the meat and let marinate at room temperature for at least 45 minutes.

Combine the lettuce, tomatoes, scallions, and cucumber in a large salad bowl and toss with the reserved dressing. Remove the steak strips from the marinade and add to the salad. Gently toss until well combined. Sprinkle with additional cilantro and serve.

Per serving: 446 calories, 26 g protein, 13 g carbohydrates, 32 g total fat, 8 g saturated fat, 71 mg cholesterol, 3 g dietary fiber, 325 mg sodium

Cooking Steak

Sautéed Steak

Heat 1 tablespoon oil in a nonstick pan over medium-high heat. Add a 1"-thick steak and cook, turning once, until browned well, about 6 minutes. Reduce the heat and continue cooking until a thermometer inserted in the center reaches 145°F for medium-rare, 3 to 4 minutes longer.

Grilled or Broiled Steak

Prepare a medium-hot grill or grill pan or preheat the broiler. Grill or broil a 1"-thick steak, turning once, until a thermometer inserted in the center reaches 145°F for medium-rare, about 10 minutes.

Steak and Tomato Salad with Horseradish Dressing

If you like strong, distinctive flavors, such as horseradish and onion, this is the salad for you! Short on time? Substitute ½ pound deli sliced roast beef for the steak. Blue cheese makes a good addition to the salad, too. Horseradish has a strong and pungent flavor, so be careful to add a little at a time to the dressing and taste as you go.

Serves 4 as an entrée

1 tablespoon olive oil

1½ cups halved cherry tomatoes (about 16)

6 fresh basil leaves, torn into pieces

1¼ pounds green beans, trimmed

Horseradish Dressing

8 cups torn romaine or mixed lettuces

½ cup thinly sliced radishes

¼ cup chopped red onion

Salt and pepper to taste

1 pound thinly sliced cooked steak (see page 109)

In a large bowl, drizzle the oil over the cherry tomatoes, add the basil, and stir gently. Set aside.

Bring about 1" of water to a boil in the bottom of a steamer or saucepan. Put the beans in the steamer basket, place over the boiling water, cover, and steam until crisp-tender, 6 to 7 minutes. Refresh under cold running water and drain. Transfer to a second bowl. Add about half of the horseradish dressing and toss to coat.

Add the lettuce, radishes, and onion to the tomatoes. Season lightly with salt and pepper and toss. Arrange on a platter. Spoon the beans on top, and arrange the beef on top of the beans. Drizzle the remaining dressing over the beef and serve.

Per serving: 392 calories, 29 g protein, 21 g carbohydrates, 21 g total fat, 6 g saturated fat, 58 mg cholesterol, 9 g dietary fiber, 297 mg sodium

Horseradish Dressing

Serves 4

¼ cup reduced-fat sour cream

¼ cup reduced-fat mayonnaise

2 tablespoons drained prepared horseradish

1 tablespoon fresh lemon juice

1 tablespoon olive oil

1 tablespoon water

Pepper to taste

Whisk together all of the ingredients in a small bowl until well combined.

Wiley's Wisdom

Many of the salads in this book are appropriate for low-carbohydrate diets. Here is a list of low-carb winners that you might want to consider including in your next salad:

- Asparagus
- Bean sprouts
- Berries
- Broccoli
- Cabbage
- Cantaloupe
- Cucumber
- Lettuce
- Mushrooms
- Mustard greens
- Radishes
- Spinach
- Strawberries
- Tomatoes
- Watermelon

Toasted Cauliflower and Roast Beef Salad

Although white in color and mild in taste, with all of its cancer-fighting properties, cauliflower is anything but bland. Here it's toasted to bring out its nutty taste. By slicing the larger cauliflower florets and cooking them in a sauté pan, you "toast" the cauliflower to a golden brown color, which brings out—and intensifies—the flavor of the vegetable. Use leftover roast beef or steak, or buy a slice of roast beef at the deli counter that's been cut on the thickest setting of the slicer. To make this a vegetarian salad, omit the roast beef and add one (15.5-ounce) can of drained and rinsed red beans.

Serves 4 as an entrée

1 head cauliflower, cored and cut into florets

6 tablespoons olive oil

Salt and pepper to taste

½ cup water

½ pound roast beef, cubed (1 cup)

1 red bell pepper, seeded and cut into thin strips

1 large carrot, shredded on the large holes of a grater

⅓ cup raisins or golden raisins

⅓ cup firmly packed torn pieces fresh basil, or 2 tablespoons dried basil

¼ cup chopped celery

½ cup apple juice

Juice of ½ lemon

2 tablespoons white wine vinegar or apple cider vinegar

One 9-ounce bag Italian lettuce mix

Slice the larger cauliflower florets ¼" thick. Heat 1 tablespoon of the oil in a large, nonstick skillet over medium-high heat. Add the cauliflower and sprinkle with salt. Add the water, cover, and simmer until the water evaporates, 3 to 4 minutes; the cauliflower should be almost cooked through. Uncover and cook, shaking the pan now and then and turning the heat down if the cauliflower begins to scorch, until the cauliflower has begun to brown, 4 to 5 minutes longer.

In a shallow bowl, combine the cauliflower, roast beef, red pepper, carrot, raisins, basil, and celery.

In a separate bowl, whisk together the apple juice, lemon juice, vinegar, and remaining 5 tablespoons oil. Season with salt and pepper. Pour over the salad and toss. Divide the lettuce among 4 plates or arrange on a serving platter. Spoon the salad and juices over and serve.

Per serving: 402 calories, 21 g protein, 28 g carbohydrates, 25 g total fat, 4 g saturated fat, 46 mg cholesterol, 7 g dietary fiber, 180 mg sodium

Roast Beef Hash Salad

My mom always used to make hash with any leftover roast beef she might have had on hand. It was a great way to spread out a little bit of meat but still leave us feeling satisfied. This hearty "steak and potatoes" salad is also a good way to use up the end of roast beef. Or just buy a thick slice at the supermarket deli and cut it into cubes.

Serves 4 as an entrée

½ pound carrots, peeled and cut into ½"-thick slices

½ pound small turnips, peeled and cut into wedges

½ pound small new potatoes, scrubbed and quartered

4 ribs celery, cut into 2" pieces

1 small red onion, cut into 8 wedges

9 tablespoons olive oil

Salt and pepper to taste

1½ tablespoons red wine vinegar

1½ teaspoons Dijon mustard

8 cups sturdy greens such as watercress, frisée, arugula, and/or baby spinach

2 cups cubed cooked beef, such as leftover steak (see page 109) or roast beef, or deli roast beef

1 cup grape tomatoes or halved cherry tomatoes

¼ cup chopped fresh parsley, or 1 tablespoon dried

Preheat the oven to 425°F. On a sheet pan, toss the carrots, turnips, potatoes, celery, and onion with 3 tablespoons of the olive oil and salt and pepper. Roast, stirring twice during cooking for even browning, until the vegetables are tender and browned, 30 to 35 minutes. Let cool 10 minutes.

Whisk together the vinegar and mustard in a large bowl. Whisk in the remaining 6 tablespoons oil and season with salt and pepper. Add the roasted vegetables, greens, beef, tomatoes, and parsley. Toss to combine and serve.

Per serving: 489 calories, 21 g protein, 23 g carbohydrates, 36 g total fat, 6 g saturated fat, 31 mg cholesterol, 6 g dietary fiber, 313 mg sodium

Wiley's Wisdom

Garlic offers a delicious taste, but sometimes it can be lingering or overpowering in a salad. To add just a whiff of that delicious fresh taste of garlic to your salad, cut a clove in half and rub the inside of your salad bowl with a cut side. You will enjoy a hint of garlic throughout the salad. You can also rub your wooden salad utensils with cut garlic, and the cutting board before chopping your vegetables.

Roll Tide Tailgate Salad

Alabamians take their college football seriously, and their tailgating even more seriously! They pull into the parking lot of the University of Alabama's Bryant-Denny Stadium, home of the Crimson Tide football team, starting the day *before* the big game to get their barbecue going. I know that my friends Bob and Liz Winter are there each Saturday—they haven't missed a home game in more than 20 years. You can find them among the thousands of other fans, eating barbecue and serving pound cake to anyone who'll stop and talk. This salad reminds me of the delicious pork barbecue dishes that are served during these tailgates. It is similar to North Carolina–style pulled pork, but is made with pork tenderloin, a much leaner cut of meat. The dressing keeps the meat moist and juicy. This recipe requires only half of a 1-pound tenderloin—use the other half for Pork and Sauerkraut Salad (page 120), Santa Fe Salad (page 118), or South of the Border Salad with Jalapeño-Lime Dressing (page 116).

Serves 4 as an entrée

½ teaspoon light brown sugar

¼ teaspoon dry mustard

¼ teaspoon garlic powder

¼ teaspoon ground sweet paprika

Salt and pepper to taste

½ pound pork tenderloin

One 9-ounce package frozen lima beans

1 small green cabbage, shredded (about 5 cups)

1 small red onion, thinly sliced (about 1 cup)

2 large carrots, shredded (about 1 cup)

Barbecue Dressing

Combine the sugar, mustard, garlic powder, paprika, and salt and pepper in a small bowl. Rub the spice mixture all over the pork. Set aside at room temperature for 10 minutes.

Prepare a medium-hot grill or grill pan or preheat the broiler. Grill or broil the tenderloin, turning once, until a thermometer inserted in the center reaches 155°F and the juices run clear, about 20 minutes. Remove from the heat, cover with foil, and let cool.

Bring about 1" of water to a boil in the bottom of a steamer or saucepan. Put the lima beans in the steamer basket, place over the boiling water, cover, and steam 2 minutes to thaw. Drain, refresh under cold running water, and drain again.

Combine the lima beans, cabbage, onion, and carrots in a large bowl. Chop the cooled pork into ½" cubes and add to the bowl. Toss everything with the dressing until well-coated and serve.

Per serving: 276 calories, 49 g protein, 34 g carbohydrates, 7 g total fat, 2 g saturated fat, 42 mg cholesterol, 8 g dietary fiber, 464 mg sodium

Barbecue Dressing

Serves 4

⅓ cup apple cider vinegar

¼ cup reduced-fat mayonnaise

2 tablespoons ketchup

1 teaspoon light brown sugar

½ teaspoon Worcestershire sauce

Salt and pepper to taste

Whisk all of the ingredients together in a bowl until well combined.

A WORD ABOUT WELLNESS

Herbs and spices are more than just powerful taste enhancers. Scientists now know that they have significant health benefits on their own, primarily because they contain valuable concentrations of flavonoids such as quercetin, which has been linked to cardiovascular health, and volatile oil phytochemicals, which contribute unique aromas and also their antioxidant potential. Ginger contains anti-inflammatory compounds, volatile oils, and antioxidants that can help the body detoxify carcinogens and protect cell membranes; cinnamon stimulates circulation and lowers blood sugar; black pepper may improve digestion and relieve nausea. Recent cancer studies that paired certain spices with plant foods and implanted them in tumors suggest that the interaction could result in cancer protection. More research is under way, but signs indicate that using as many spices and herbs as you can in combination with your favorite fruits and vegetables is a good health move as well as a flavor sensation.

South of the Border Salad with Jalapeño-Lime Dressing

This spicy salad is wonderful on its own or stuffed inside a tortilla. The recipe calls for only half of a 1-pound pork tenderloin. The remaining half can be used in Pork and Sauerkraut Salad (page 120), Santa Fe Salad (page 118), or Roll Tide Tailgate Salad (page 114).

Serves 4 as an entrée

½ pound pork tenderloin

⅛ teaspoon ground cinnamon

Salt and pepper to taste

2 tablespoons canola oil

1 small red onion, thinly sliced (about 1 cup)

2 tablespoons raisins

8 cups bite-size pieces romaine or green leaf lettuce

1 large green bell pepper, seeded and diced

1 large tomato, diced

1 medium avocado, halved, pitted, peeled, and diced

⅓ cup thinly sliced radishes (about 4 radishes)

Jalapeño-Lime Dressing

4 flour or corn tortillas

Sprinkle the pork with the cinnamon and salt and pepper and rub all over. Heat the oil in a nonstick skillet over medium heat. Add the pork and cook for 10 minutes. Turn the pork, add the onion, and cook until a thermometer inserted in the center of the pork reaches 155°F and the juices run clear, 10 minutes longer. Add the raisins and cook, stirring gently, until the raisins are plump, 1 to 2 minutes. Remove the pan from the heat and let the pork rest for 10 minutes. Slice the pork into ½"-thick pieces.

Combine the lettuce, bell pepper, tomato, avocado, and radishes in a large mixing bowl and toss well with the dressing.

To serve, divide the salad among 4 plates or shallow bowls. Arrange the sliced pork, onions, and raisins on top. Warm the tortillas in a dry skillet for 1 minute or the microwave for 30 seconds and serve alongside.

Per serving: 429 calories, 15 g protein, 18 g carbohydrates, 35 g total fat, 4 g saturated fat, 37 mg cholesterol, 7 g dietary fiber, 195 mg sodium

Jalapeño-Lime Dressing

Serves 4

⅓ cup canola oil

¼ cup fresh lime juice (from 2 limes)

2 teaspoons minced fresh jalapeño chile pepper (from ½ jalapeño; wear plastic gloves when handling)

Salt and pepper to taste

Whisk all of the ingredients together in a bowl until well combined.

Santa Fe Salad

I always look forward to attending the annual Santa Fe Festival held each September. Most of the tourists have gone home by then, and the festival pays tribute to the local residents and culture. Food plays a big part in the celebration, and in the past I've sampled some wonderful fresh local salads, like the ones that inspired this one. Cumin is a ground dried spice often found in Mexican and Indian food. Here it is used to flavor the pork. This recipe calls for only half of a 1-pound pork tenderloin. The remaining half can be used in South of the Border Salad with Jalapeño-Lime Dressing (page 116) or Roll Tide Tailgate Salad (page 114).

Serves 4 as an entrée

½ pound pork tenderloin

¼ teaspoon ground cumin

Salt and pepper to taste

1 ear corn, husked, or ¾ cup corn kernels

1 teaspoon canola oil (optional)

8 cups baby spinach

One 15.5-ounce can black beans, drained and rinsed

1 cucumber, peeled and diced

1 cup diced Granny Smith apple (1 small)

2 scallions (green and white parts), thinly sliced

Chipotle Dressing

Sprinkle the pork with the cumin and salt and pepper and rub all over. Set aside at room temperature while the grill heats.

Prepare a medium-hot grill or grill pan. Grill the tenderloin, turning once, until a thermometer inserted in the center reaches 155°F and the juices run clear, about 20 minutes. Remove from the heat, cover with foil, and let cool. Cut into bite-size pieces.

If using fresh corn, rub the oil all over the corn. Grill, turning occasionally, until nicely browned on all sides, about 9 minutes. Remove from the heat and let cool. Cut the kernels off the cob (see page 50).

Combine the pork, corn, spinach, black beans, cucumber, apple, and scallions in a large bowl. Add the dressing and toss until well combined. Serve immediately.

Per serving: 256 calories, 19 g protein, 28 g carbohydrates, 10 g total fat, 2 g saturated fat, 43 mg cholesterol, 8 g dietary fiber, 541 mg sodium

Chipotle Dressing

This makes a small amount of dressing, but it's quite powerful, so a little goes a long way. For a milder dressing, cut the amount of chipotle chile pepper in half.

1 chipotle chile pepper packed in adobo sauce

¼ cup reduced-fat sour cream

1 tablespoon canola oil

1 teaspoon red wine vinegar

Salt and pepper to taste

Remove the stem from the chile and split in half lengthwise. Scrape out and discard the seeds and veins and mince the chile. Whisk together the minced chile, sour cream, oil, vinegar, and salt and pepper in a small bowl.

Wiley's Wisdom

Chipotles are smoked and dried jalapeños. I love the flavor that they add to food. Their smoky flavor and natural pepper sweetness is complementary to just about anything that they are combined with. If dried chipotles are not available, use jarred. Chipotle chiles in adobo sauce are smoked jalapeño chiles that are canned in a thick tomato sauce. Both the chile and the sauce are fiery hot. Once the can has been opened, the chiles can be refrigerated for 2 to 3 weeks, or frozen for 3 months. To make a great-tasting vinaigrette, add chipotle sparingly to your favorite oil and vinegar dressing.

Pork and Sauerkraut Salad

Oh, what a meal! This salad really is a meal unto itself with flavorful roasted pork set atop a bed of spinach. Pork tenderloin is a very lean cut, but if you prefer, you can substitute 1 cup diced, cooked, boneless, skinless, white-meat chicken. This recipe requires only half of a 1-pound tenderloin—use the other half for Roll Tide Tailgate Salad (page 114), South of the Border Salad with Jalapeño-Lime Dressing (page 116), or Santa Fe Salad (page 118).

Serves 4 as an entrée

2 small yams

½ pound pork tenderloin

Salt and pepper

8 cups baby spinach

3 cups prepared sauerkraut, rinsed and squeezed dry

2 cups ½"-diced dried apples

1 cup dried cranberries

Honey Dressing

Preheat the oven to 400°F. Prick the yams with a fork, place on a foil-lined baking sheet, and roast until very soft, 45 to 50 minutes. Let cool. Peel and cut into cubes.

Prepare a medium-hot grill or grill pan or preheat the broiler. Sprinkle the tenderloin with salt and pepper. Grill or broil the tenderloin, turning once, until a thermometer inserted in the center reaches 155°F and the juices run clear, about 20 minutes. Remove from the heat, cover with foil, and let cool. Cut into bite-size pieces.

In a bowl, combine the sweet potatoes, pork, spinach, sauerkraut, apples, cranberries, and dressing and toss.

Per serving: 722 calories, 20 g protein, 117 g carbohydrates, 21 g total fat, 3 g saturated fat, 45 mg cholesterol, 14 g dietary fiber, 1,988 mg sodium

Honey Dressing

Serves 4

⅓ cup olive oil

¼ cup red wine vinegar

2 tablespoons honey

2 teaspoons chopped fresh thyme, or ¼ teaspoon dried

Salt and pepper to taste

Whisk together all of the ingredients in a small bowl until well combined.

BLT Salad

Whenever I think of BLTs, I think back to when my college roommate Buddy Bell and I would sneak off to Johnny's Grill in Tuscaloosa for the best BLTs around. This salad is just as appealing and delicious as those beloved sandwiches. The only thing missing here is the extra calories.

Serves 4 as an entrée

8 strips turkey bacon

4 slices whole wheat bread, cut into 1" cubes

2 tablespoons olive oil

8 cups bite-size pieces mixed lettuce, or one 12-ounce bag American lettuce mix

2 beefsteak tomatoes, cut into wedges

Cooked kernels from 2 ears corn (see page 50), or 2 cups frozen corn, thawed in the microwave 1 to 2 minutes

1 avocado, halved, pitted, peeled, and sliced

Buttermilk Dressing (page 19)

Preheat the oven to 400°F. Lay the bacon strips on a baking sheet and bake, turning after 8 minutes, until crisp, about 15 minutes total. Transfer to a paper towel–lined plate to drain. Break the bacon into 1" pieces.

Toss the bread cubes in a bowl with the olive oil. Spread out on a separate baking sheet and bake until the croutons are crisp, 10 to 15 minutes.

Combine the bacon, croutons, lettuce, tomatoes, corn, and avocado in a bowl. Add the dressing, toss until combined, and serve.

Per serving: 395 calories, 12 g protein, 29 g carbohydrates, 27 g total fat, 5 g saturated fat, 38 mg cholesterol, 8 g dietary fiber, 709 mg sodium

Autumnal Solstice Salad

This salad combines the earthy, sweet flavors of spinach, mushrooms, and raisins with the saltiness of prosciutto. You can find prosciutto, a dry-cured ham from Italy, in most grocery store deli departments or refrigerated cold cut sections. You can also use 4 slices of cooked turkey bacon instead.

Serves 4 as an entrée

4 tablespoons olive oil

1 clove garlic, sliced

Needles from 1 sprig fresh rosemary, or ¼ teaspoon dried rosemary

1 teaspoon fresh thyme, or ¼ teaspoon dried

1 pound assorted mushrooms, such as white, cremini, shiitake, and portobello

2 leeks, halved, well washed, trimmed, and cut into 1" pieces (see page 57)

Salt and pepper to taste

2 sun-dried tomato halves, finely chopped

1 tablespoon balsamic vinegar

1 teaspoon reduced-sodium soy sauce

8 cups mixed greens

1 Bosc pear, cored and cut into 1" cubes

¼ cup raisins

3 tablespoons pine nuts or chopped pecans, toasted (see page 30)

4 ounces prosciutto

In a large nonstick skillet, combine 3 tablespoons of the oil and the garlic. If using fresh rosemary and fresh thyme, add them now. Cook over medium-low heat until the garlic begins to turn golden brown. Add the mushrooms and leeks, and the dried herbs if using. Reduce the heat to medium and cook, stirring every now and then, until the mushrooms produce a liquid, 2 to 3 minutes. Increase the heat to medium-high, sprinkle with salt and pepper, and cook until the liquid has evaporated, about 6 minutes longer.

Meanwhile, combine the sun-dried tomatoes, vinegar, soy sauce, and remaining 1 tablespoon oil in a medium bowl and whisk to combine. Add the greens, pear, raisins, and pine nuts or pecans.

Add the mushroom mixture to the salad and toss until well combined. Divide among 4 plates. Roll up each slice of prosciutto, distribute around the salads, and serve.

Per serving: 349 calories, 16 g protein, 29 g carbohydrates, 22 g total fat, 3 g saturated fat, 22 mg cholesterol, 6 g dietary fiber, 943 mg sodium

A WORD ABOUT WELLNESS

All lettuces and greens are mostly water and considered low-fat and low-calorie foods. Iceberg, the ubiquitous, mild-tasting, light green–colored head, is a good source of chlorophyll, vitamin K, and choline, a nutrient that works with B vitamins to metabolize fats. But in general, darker leafed greens provide more nutrients such as beta-carotene and phytochemicals, and in most cases, stronger taste. For example, 2 cups of romaine lettuce contribute 45 percent of the daily value of vitamin C. It is also loaded with vitamin A, folic acid, vitamins B_1 and B_2, and manganese and chromium. Other greens, like arugula, spinach, mustard greens, and cabbage, are members of the cruciferous family and share its high levels of cancer-fighting antioxidants.

Lentil Salad with Prosciutto

The perfect addition to a buffet table, this hearty lentil salad offers the refreshing taste of cherry tomatoes and the rich flavor of prosciutto. Keep in mind when cooking lentils that the older they are, the longer they will need to cook to become tender.

Serves 4 as an entrée

1½ cups lentils, washed, any little stones or pebbles discarded

2 carrots, peeled and cut into ¼" dice (about 1 cup)

1 onion, peeled

1 clove garlic, peeled

2 bay leaves

2 sprigs fresh thyme or ¼ teaspoon dried thyme

Salt and pepper to taste

Chive-Mustard Dressing

12 cherry tomatoes, halved

4 ounces prosciutto, torn into large pieces

3 tablespoons minced fresh parsley

Place the lentils in a 3-quart saucepan along with the carrots, onion, garlic, bay leaves, thyme, and salt and pepper. Add water to cover by 1½". Bring to a boil and cover. Reduce the heat and simmer for 15 to 30 minutes (depending on the age of the lentils), until all of the water has been absorbed and the lentils are tender. Check the lentils every so often to make sure that the water has not evaporated too soon. If lentils begin to stick, add another ¼ cup water.

Transfer the cooked lentils to a bowl and discard the onion, bay leaves, and thyme sprigs. Stir in the dressing. Let cool to room temperature. Stir in the cherry tomatoes and prosciutto. Sprinkle with the parsley and serve.

Per serving: 587 calories, 26 g protein, 52 g carbohydrates, 31 g total fat, 5 g saturated fat, 5 mg cholesterol, 24 g dietary fiber, 702 mg sodium

Chive-Mustard Dressing

Serves 4

½ cup olive oil

¼ cup red wine vinegar

2 tablespoons minced chives or shallots

1 teaspoon Dijon mustard

Whisk together all of the ingredients in a small bowl until well combined.

A WORD ABOUT WELLNESS

Apart from being able to single-handedly and together raise the flavor bar of many of our favorite recipes, garlic, onions, and other members of the allium family (which includes scallions, shallots, chives, and leeks) have been shown to protect and fight against certain cancers, such as stomach, prostate, and esophageal. One reason may be that onions and their relatives contain a compound that can increase the production of a major anticancer enzyme in your body. Sulfur phytochemicals found in onions and garlic may be able to curb or shrink the buildup of plaque in the arteries, protecting against heart attack.

Spinach Salad

Spinach is not only one of my favorite-tasting vegetables (I eat it almost every day in one form or another), it's also loaded with nutrients such as calcium, folate, vitamin A, and iron. Here it's offered in a healthier version of the classic salad.

Serves 4 as an entrée

6 slices turkey bacon

8 cups baby spinach

2 hard-cooked eggs, sliced

1 jarred roasted red pepper or homemade roasted pepper (see page 181), cut into strips

4 ounces white mushrooms, sliced (about 2 cups)

1½ cups seedless red grapes, each halved

2 scallions (green and white parts), thinly sliced

2 cups store-bought croutons, or Homemade Croutons (page 95) made with 4 slices whole wheat bread

Apple Cider Dressing

Preheat the oven to 400°F. Put the bacon on a baking sheet with sides and bake, turning once, until crisp, about 15 minutes. Transfer to a paper towel–lined plate and drain.

Combine the spinach, eggs, red pepper, mushrooms, grapes, scallions, and croutons in a bowl. Crumble in the bacon. Add the dressing, toss, and serve.

Per serving: 452 calories, 11 g protein, 34 g carbohydrates, 31 g total fat, 6 g saturated fat, 130 mg cholesterol, 4 g dietary fiber, 718 mg sodium

Apple Cider Dressing

Serves 4

3 tablespoons apple cider vinegar

3 tablespoons canola oil

3 tablespoons olive oil

1 tablespoon water

1 tablespoon sugar

½ teaspoon dried mustard

Salt and pepper to taste

Whisk together all of the ingredients in a small bowl until well combined.

"Poke Salet" with Bacon and Eggs

Whenever we used to get in the car with my Aunt Ollie, she'd always pull over to the side of the road and pick some pokeweed to make a salad called *poke salet*. "Poke," or pokeweed, is a wild green that grows in early spring and summer. It is considered to be very nutritious. This recipe uses spinach instead of poke, and a minimal amount of the traditional bacon fat if desired.

Serves 4 as an entrée

4 slices turkey bacon

One 9-ounce bag baby spinach

6 eggs

Salt and pepper to taste

5 tablespoons olive or canola oil (replace 1 tablespoon with bacon fat, if desired)

2 scallions (white and green parts), chopped

1 tablespoon red wine vinegar

1 teaspoon Dijon mustard

8 cups frisée

¾ cup grape or halved cherry tomatoes

1½ cups sliced white mushrooms

Cook the bacon in a medium nonstick skillet over medium heat until the fat is rendered and the bacon is crisp, 7 to 8 minutes. Drain on paper towels. Pour off the fat, reserving 1 tablespoon if desired.

Place the spinach in the skillet, cover, and cook over medium heat until wilted, 3 to 4 minutes. Uncover and cook 2 minutes to evaporate some of the moisture. Drain in a colander in the sink, pressing the spinach against the sides of the colander to extract as much liquid as possible. Reserve the skillet.

Whisk the eggs in a bowl with a fork. Season to taste with salt and pepper.

Heat 1 tablespoon of the olive oil or the bacon fat in the skillet over medium heat. Add the spinach and scallions and season with salt and pepper. Cook, stirring, 2 minutes. Add the eggs and cook, stirring, until scrambled and firm, about 3 minutes.

Whisk the vinegar, mustard, and remaining 4 tablespoons oil in a large bowl. Season to taste with salt and pepper. Add the frisée, tomatoes, and mushrooms and toss. Divide the salad among four plates, spoon the eggs on top, and serve.

Per serving: 336 calories, 16 g protein, 8 g carbohydrates, 28 g total fat, 6 g saturated fat, 330 mg cholesterol, 4 g dietary fiber, 437 mg sodium

Frittata Salad

A frittata is an Italian open-faced omelet cooked until the bottom is set, then inverted back into the pan or placed under a broiler to cook the top. The frittata for this wonderful brunch salad should be served warm or at room temperature.

Serves 4 as an entrée

½ pound asparagus, trimmed and cut into ½" pieces

1 tablespoon olive oil

1 medium onion, sliced (about 1 cup)

3 cups sliced mushrooms

Salt and pepper to taste

6 eggs

1 cup grated Parmesan cheese

2 tablespoons canola oil

8 cups bite-size pieces mixed greens such as escarole, radicchio, and spinach

1 green bell pepper, seeded and cut into strips

Kernels from 2 ears raw or cooked corn (see page 50), or 2 cups frozen corn, thawed in the microwave 1 to 2 minutes

10 cherry tomatoes, each halved, or 2 tomatoes, cut into chunks

Shallot Vinaigrette (page 23)

Bring a small saucepan of salted water to a boil. Add the asparagus and cook until tender but still firm and with a bright green color, about 3 minutes. Drain and set aside.

Heat the olive oil in a 9" nonstick skillet over very low heat. Add the onion and cook until wilted and golden, 10 to 15 minutes. Add 2 cups of the mushrooms and sauté until wilted, about 5 minutes. Season with salt and pepper. Remove the vegetables from the pan and allow them to cool for a few minutes. Reserve the skillet to cook the eggs in.

Beat the eggs in a bowl with a fork. Add the cooked asparagus, onion, and mushrooms and the Parmesan. Season lightly with salt and pepper. Heat the canola oil over medium heat in the nonstick skillet. Add the egg mixture, reduce the heat to very low, and cook without stirring until the eggs set on the bottom, about 10 minutes. Place a large, flat dinner plate over the skillet and overturn the skillet and plate so that the frittata falls onto the plate, cooked side up. Slide the frittata back into the pan, cooked side up, and cook just long enough to set the eggs, 1 to 2 minutes longer. Transfer to a platter and cut into 8 wedges.

In a large bowl, combine the greens, bell pepper, remaining 1 cup mushrooms, the corn, tomatoes, and vinaigrette. Toss and divide among 4 large plates. Arrange 2 wedges of frittata on top of each and serve.

Per serving: 318 calories, 20 g protein, 7 g carbohydrates, 24 g total fat, 7 g saturated fat, 335 mg cholesterol, 2 g dietary fiber, 415 mg sodium

Grilled Tofu and Asparagus Salad

Grilling is a wonderful way to cook tofu, as it picks up the charred, smoky flavors quite well. Use extra-firm tofu for this recipe because it will remain intact.

Serves 4 as an entrée

One 8-ounce package extra-firm tofu, cut into 1" cubes

2 red onions, cut into 1" chunks

2 tablespoons canola oil

Salt and pepper to taste

1 bunch asparagus, trimmed (1 pound)

8 cups chopped iceberg or romaine lettuce

2 tomatoes, cored and cut into wedges

Carrot-Ginger Dressing (page 39)

Soak 8 bamboo skewers in cold water for 30 minutes. Prepare a medium-hot grill or grill pan. Thread the tofu and onion pieces onto the skewers, alternating tofu with onion. Place on a baking sheet and drizzle with 1 tablespoon of the oil. Season with salt and pepper. Toss the asparagus with the remaining oil on the sheet pan and season with salt and pepper.

Grill the skewers and asparagus spears, turning occasionally, until the tofu is evenly browned and the asparagus charred and wrinkled, about 12 minutes. Cool slightly. Remove the tofu and onions from the skewers; cut the asparagus in half.

Divide the lettuce among 4 bowls. Top with the tofu, onions, asparagus, and tomatoes. Drizzle with the dressing and serve.

Per serving: 297 calories, 11 g protein, 26 g carbohydrates, 22 g total fat, 1 g saturated fat, 0 mg cholesterol, 6 g dietary fiber, 89 mg sodium

A WORD ABOUT WELLNESS

Soybeans and soy foods such as tofu are associated with an unusually large number of healthful properties. But critics warn that soy may not be for everyone because of risks of allergies, thyroid problems, and some cancers, especially from processed soy. Natural soy is nature's only complete non-animal protein, and most of its benefits, such as its ability to lower LDLs (bad cholesterol) without reducing HDLs (good cholesterol), derive from that. Essential fatty acids, phytosterols, and lecithin support these cholesterol-lowering properties as well as cancer-fighting abilities. Soybeans are a good source of dietary fiber, which aids in digestion and elimination and in maintaining cholesterol and blood sugar levels. Isoflavonoids, of which soy is the major source, may relieve some postmenopausal symptoms and bone loss in women, as well as protect cardiovascular health and retard tumor growth.

Tofu Salad
with Sesame Dressing

Tofu is made by curdling soy milk, then draining and pressing the curds, similar to the way cheese is made. It's sold in a variety of textures, from extra firm to soft—the firmer, the less water is in the curd, and the more protein. Firm tofu is a good choice for salads because it holds together well. Once open, store leftover tofu covered in water in the refrigerator and use within a few days.

Serves 4 as an entrée

1 pound string beans, trimmed and cut into 1" pieces

Sesame Dressing

One 15-ounce block firm tofu, cut into ½" dice

1 cup chopped scallions (white and green parts)

8 cups mixed greens

Bring about 1" of water to a boil in the bottom of a steamer or saucepan. Put the beans in the steamer basket, place over the boiling water, cover, and steam until crisp-tender, 6 to 7 minutes. Refresh under cold running water and drain.

Whisk the dressing in a large bowl. Add the beans, tofu, and scallions and toss. Serve at room temperature on a bed of greens.

Per serving: 341 calories, 21 g protein, 19 g carbohydrates, 24 g total fat, 3 g saturated fat, 0 mg cholesterol, 10 g dietary fiber, 713 mg sodium

Sesame Dressing

Serves 4

5 tablespoons reduced-sodium soy sauce

¼ cup sesame oil

¾ teaspoon sugar

Whisk together all of the ingredients in a small bowl until combined.

Toasting Sesame Seeds

Toast sesame seeds in a small skillet over low heat, shaking the pan often for even browning, until fragrant, 3 to 4 minutes.

Roasted Spring Vegetable Salad

Asparagus and new potatoes are at the height of their season in early to mid-spring. Roasting helps bring out even more deep flavor in these tender vegetables. This salad can be served as an entrée on its own, or alongside grilled lamb or fish.

Serves 4 as an entrée

3 bunches large radishes, trimmed and quartered (2¼ pounds)

1½ pounds new potatoes, scrubbed and quartered

2 cloves garlic, crushed with the side of a large knife

Salt and pepper to taste

¼ cup + 1 tablespoon olive oil

1 bunch asparagus, trimmed (1 pound)

8 cups mixed greens

2 cups (10 ounces) frozen green peas, heated in a steamer or microwave to thaw

Lemon-Dill Dressing

Preheat the oven to 450°F. Combine the radishes, potatoes, and garlic in a roasting pan large enough to hold them in a single layer. Sprinkle with salt and pepper and drizzle with ¼ cup of the oil. Toss until everything is evenly coated. Roast, stirring every 10 minutes, until the vegetables are tender, about 35 minutes. Let cool.

Meanwhile, place the asparagus on a rimmed baking sheet, sprinkle with salt and pepper, and drizzle with the remaining 1 tablespoon oil. Toss until well coated. Roast until slightly browned, about 10 minutes. Let cool and cut into 1" lengths.

Combine the asparagus, greens, and peas in a large mixing bowl. Add the dressing and toss. Divide the salad among 4 plates or shallow bowls, top with the radish and potato mixture, and serve.

Per serving: 447 calories, 12 g protein, 33 g carbohydrates, 31 g total fat, 4 g saturated fat, 0 mg cholesterol, 15 g dietary fiber, 358 mg sodium

Lemon-Dill Dressing

Serves 4

¼ cup fresh lemon juice (1 large lemon)

¼ cup olive oil

¼ cup minced dill (3 sprigs)

Salt and pepper to taste

Whisk all of the ingredients together in a bowl until well combined.

Tomato Salad with Squash, Ricotta, and Pesto Dressing

This Italian-inspired summer salad takes advantage of a variety of things found in abundance in the garden, including ripe tomatoes, basil, and squash. Pesto is a flavorful Italian sauce of pureed fresh basil, garlic, olive oil, and pine nuts. The pesto can also be served alongside grilled meat, chicken, and fish, or tossed with whole grain pasta.

Serves 4 as an entrée

1 small zucchini, peeled into long, thin ribbons with a vegetable peeler

1 small yellow squash, peeled into long, thin ribbons with a vegetable peeler, seeded core discarded

1 pound ripe tomatoes, any kind, including beefsteak, cherry, grape, or plum; large tomatoes cut into wedges, cherry tomatoes halved (if large) or left whole

1 cup part-skim ricotta cheese

Pesto Dressing

Fresh basil leaves

Arrange a bed of zucchini and squash ribbons on each of 4 plates. Scatter the tomatoes on top. Add the ricotta cheese by spoonfuls. Drizzle all over with the dressing, garnish with fresh basil leaves, and serve.

Per serving: 293 calories, 9 g protein, 11 g carbohydrates, 25 g total fat, 6 g saturated fat, 19 mg cholesterol, 3 g dietary fiber, 160 mg sodium

Pesto Dressing

Serves 4

1 cup firmly packed basil leaves (from 1 small bunch)

⅓ cup olive oil

1 tablespoon pine nuts or walnuts

½ (or 1 very small) clove garlic, smashed with the side of a large knife, peeled, and roughly chopped

Salt and pepper to taste

Combine all of the ingredients in a small food processor or blender and process until smooth.

A WORD ABOUT WELLNESS

What you put on your salad may be as important, if not more important, as what you put into it. As you know, most salad dressings contain some kind of oil or fat to bind their flavorings, give them texture, and help the dressing adhere to the salad ingredients themselves. Fats in oil can even promote the absorption of nutrients such as lycopene in a tomato salad. Studies show that using extra virgin olive oil will not only give you a great-tasting dressing, but it can deliver major health benefits as well. One reason is that extra virgin olive oil contains polyphenols, powerful antioxidants that block the formation of cancer cells and protect against heart disease. It is also rich in monounsaturated fats, the most important being oleic acid, which has been credited with lowering triglyceride levels and raising HDL cholesterol levels. Other healthful monounsaturated oils include canola oil and peanut oil.

Whole Wheat Bread and Vegetable Salad

This salad is inspired by *panzanella*, an Italian bread salad. It is particularly nice with a dense whole wheat or multigrain bread, but a sliced store-bought whole wheat or two 7-inch pitas will work too. You can prepare the salad ahead, as it will last overnight in the refrigerator. Allow it to come to room temperature before serving.

Serves 4 as an entrée

2 pounds tomatoes, cored and diced

Salt and pepper to taste

4 cups cubed whole wheat or multigrain bread (about 3 thick slices)

1 tablespoon olive oil

¾ cup fresh basil leaves, torn into small pieces, or 1 tablespoon dried basil

⅓ cup chopped red onion

2 small ribs celery, sliced (about ½ cup)

1 cucumber, peeled and diced

¼ honeydew melon, cut into large dice

Garlicky Dressing

8 cups sliced romaine, Boston, or Bibb lettuce

Preheat the oven to 400°F. Combine the tomatoes and ½ teaspoon salt in a large bowl and let stand while you make the rest of the salad.

Toss the bread cubes with the oil and place on a baking sheet in a single layer. Bake until lightly browned, about 10 minutes. Let cool.

Add the bread cubes to the bowl with the tomatoes, along with the basil, onion, celery, cucumber, melon, and dressing. Season with salt and pepper and toss. Let stand 1 hour to let the flavors combine.

To serve, add the lettuce and toss.

Per serving: 375 calories, 7 g protein, 39 g carbohydrates, 23 g total fat, 3 g saturated fat, 0 mg cholesterol, 9 g dietary fiber, 238 mg sodium

Garlicky Dressing

Serves 4

¼ cup red wine vinegar

5 tablespoons olive oil

2 tablespoons water

1 clove garlic, pressed through a garlic press or mashed with the side of a large knife on a cutting board

Whisk together all of the ingredients in a small bowl until well combined.

Wiley's Wisdom

All of us like to prepare ahead of time, particularly if we are having someone to dinner. But if you want the maximum nutritional advantages from salads, always wait to prepare them until just before serving. Cutting, tearing, or exposing the flesh of fruits and vegetables to light or air can easily and quickly cause valuable nutrients to be lost. For instance, it's possible for produce that has been cut to lose 100 percent of its vitamin C content within an hour or so after it was exposed to the elements.

Stuffed Bell Pepper Salad

Late summer always signaled the arrival of an abundance of bell peppers in my grandmother's garden. She would make these stuffed peppers at least once a week to help use them up. You can make the dish with green bell peppers, but because they are somewhat bitter, I recommend red or yellow. You can chop the tops of the peppers and add to the rice mixture if you like, or store them in the refrigerator and add them to another salad. For a nonvegetarian option, try sautéing ground turkey and adding it to the rice mixture.

Serves 4 as an entrée

¾ cup brown rice

1¾ cups water

Salt and pepper to taste

4 red, yellow, or green bell peppers

Cooked kernels from 1 ear corn (see page 50), or 1 cup frozen corn, thawed in the microwave 1 to 2 minutes

⅓ cup currants or raisins

⅓ cup pecans, toasted (see page 30) and chopped

¼ cup chopped red onion

¼ cup chopped fresh cilantro, or 2 teaspoons dried

3 tablespoons olive oil

Juice of ½ lemon

8 cups bite-size pieces mixed greens, or one 12-ounce bag Veggie Lover's salad mix

One 15.5-ounce can black beans, drained and rinsed

Shallot–Red Wine Vinaigrette

1 cup shredded Cheddar or Monterey Jack cheese

Combine the rice, water, and salt in a saucepan. Bring to a boil and reduce the heat to very low. Cover and cook until the rice is tender and the water has evaporated, 30 to 40 minutes. Let stand off heat for 10 minutes.

Meanwhile, slice the tops off the peppers. Remove and discard the stems and seeds. Use a spoon to scrape out the white pith. Chop the tops and add to the rice mixture if you like; or wrap and refrigerate for another use.

Preheat the oven to 400°F. In a large bowl, combine the chopped peppers if using, the corn, currants or raisins, pecans, onion, cilantro, oil, and lemon juice and season with salt and pepper. Spoon the rice mixture into the peppers.

Stand the peppers in a greased baking dish and cover with aluminum foil. Bake until the peppers are very tender, about 50 minutes. Remove the foil and bake 5 minutes longer.

Combine the lettuce, black beans, and about three-quarters of the dressing in a bowl and toss. Divide among 4 plates or shallow bowls. Set a pepper on top of each salad and cut open to expose the rice. Drizzle the remaining dressing over the peppers, sprinkle with the cheese, and serve.

Per serving: 736 calories, 20 g protein, 67 g carbohydrates, 46 g total fat, 11 g saturated fat, 30 mg cholesterol, 14 g dietary fiber, 603 mg sodium

Shallot–Red Wine Vinaigrette

Serves 4

¼ cup + 1 tablespoon olive oil

2 tablespoons red wine vinegar

1 tablespoon water

1 shallot, minced

Salt and pepper to taste

Whisk together all of the ingredients in a small bowl until well combined.

A WORD ABOUT WELLNESS

Sweet bell peppers come in an array of bright colors and are dense with nutrients such as vitamin C, beta-carotene, vitamin K, folic acid, and vitamin B_6—they are also very low in calories. Red bell peppers, which are fully ripened green peppers, have a sweeter flavor and higher nutritional profile than green. Red peppers have three times as much vitamin C as green and eleven times more beta-carotene. However, green peppers do have twice the amount of vitamin C by weight as citrus fruits. Due to their high levels of antioxidants, bell peppers have been shown to protect against cataracts, prevent blood clots, and reduce the risks of heart attack and stroke. Lycopene, a probable cancer-fighting phytochemical that is found rarely in food, is found in red bell peppers.

Pesto Pasta Salad with Grilled Vegetables

The sweet taste of basil pesto is combined here with the smoky flavors of grilled peppers, onion, and squash. If you don't have an outdoor grill available, a good alternative is a cast iron, stovetop grill pan. Its flat, ridged surface holds heat well, browning food with minimal fat, and contributes a terrific, caramelized taste.

Serves 4 as an entrée

1 eggplant, about ¾ pound, trimmed and cut into ½"-thick rounds

½ pound small zucchini or yellow squash, trimmed and cut in half lengthwise

1 red bell pepper, quartered and seeded

½ red onion, cut crosswise into ¼"-thick rounds

1–2 tablespoons olive oil, for brushing

Salt and pepper to taste

½ lemon

8 ounces fusilli or other pasta, preferably whole grain

Pesto Dressing (page 133)

½ cup grated Parmesan cheese

Prepare a medium-hot grill or grill pan. Place the eggplant, zucchini, red pepper, and onion on a baking sheet or platter in a single layer. Brush with the oil and sprinkle with salt and pepper. Working in batches, place the vegetables on the grill, oiled side down. Brush with more oil and sprinkle with salt and pepper. Grill until softened and well browned: 3 to 5 minutes each side for the eggplant, about 5 minutes each side for the squash, 3 to 4 minutes each side for the pepper, and 4 to 5 minutes each side for the onion.

As they finish cooking, transfer the vegetables to a cutting board. Cut the zucchini and pepper into 1" to 1½" pieces. Combine the vegetables in a large bowl and squeeze the lemon over.

Cook the pasta in a large pot of boiling, salted water until al dente as directed on the package. Drain in a colander.

Add the pasta to the bowl with the vegetables along with the dressing and toss gently. Taste for seasoning. Serve at room temperature, sprinkled with the Parmesan.

Per serving: *524 calories, 13 g protein, 52 g carbohydrates, 26 g total fat, 6 g saturated fat, 0 mg cholesterol, 9 g dietary fiber, 244 mg sodium*

Wiley's Wisdom

One of the biggest pitfalls that some of us experience is eating too much of these delicious healthy foods. We all know that beans, potatoes, fish, and fresh fruit are good for us. However, we can have too much of a good thing. Watch those serving sizes and don't overdo the carbs. Portion control is key. You can load up your body with sugar without even having dessert. For example, potatoes and white rice are naturally fat-free foods and they are good for you. However, they are starchy foods, and their starches are quickly converted to sugar once they are inside your body. Remember this: Knowing your food is just as important as knowing your portion sizes. Here's a quick guide to help you measure your servings of starch:

- 1 slice of bread is a serving.
- 1 small potato is a serving.
- ½ cup cooked cereal (like oatmeal) is a serving.
- ¾ cup dry cereal flakes (like cornflakes or Wheaties) is a serving.
- 1 small tortilla wrap is a serving.

Lima Bean and Broccoli Salad with Honey-Mustard Vinaigrette

This is a wonderful vegetarian entrée salad. The recipe calls for 4 cups of broccoli, but if you prefer you can use 4 cups of prepared broccoli slaw, which is found in the produce aisle of your grocery store. No need to cook the slaw, as you would the broccoli—just incorporate it raw into the salad.

Serves 4 as an entrée

2 heads broccoli, cut into florets

One 9-ounce package frozen lima beans

¾ cup chopped red bell pepper

¾ cup chopped green bell pepper

¼ cup walnut pieces, toasted (see page 30)

2 scallions (white and green parts), thinly sliced

½ jalapeño chile pepper, seeded and minced (wear plastic gloves when handling)

Salt and pepper to taste

Honey-Mustard Vinaigrette (page 96)

8 cups baby spinach

3 ounces Cheddar cheese, grated

Bring about 1" water to a boil in the bottom of a steamer or saucepan. Put the broccoli florets in the steamer basket, place over the boiling water, cover, and steam until the broccoli is just tender, 5 to 6 minutes. Drain in a colander, cool under cold running water, and drain again. Transfer to a large bowl. Add the lima beans to the steamer and steam 2 minutes to thaw. Drain, run under cold water, and drain again.

Add the lima beans to the bowl with the broccoli, along with the red pepper, green pepper, walnuts, scallions, and jalapeño. Season with salt and pepper and toss. Add the vinaigrette and toss again.

Make a bed of spinach leaves on each of 4 plates. Spoon the salad on top, sprinkle with the grated cheese, and serve.

Per serving: *500 calories, 21 g protein, 43 g carbohydrates, 26 g total fat, 7 g saturated fat, 35 mg cholesterol, 16 g dietary fiber, 404 mg sodium*

A WORD ABOUT WELLNESS

Many experts recommend eating a handful (about ¼ cup) of nuts and seeds at least five times a week for a host of health benefits. One study showed that people who did just that cut their risk of heart attack in half compared with those who consumed less than one serving a week. Nuts and seeds are important sources of heart-healthy omega-3 fatty acids (walnuts are particularly loaded with them), vitamin E (almonds are the best nut source of all), fiber (there is more fiber in a serving of pistachio nuts than in ½ cup broccoli), and protein (¼ cup almonds contains almost 8 grams of protein, more than a large egg), along with vitamin B and heart-healthy monounsaturated fats. Nut oils also provide important antioxidant and monounsaturated fat benefits. For example, macadamia nut oil is four and a half times richer in vitamin E, and its "good fat" content (85 percent) is higher, than that of olive oil. Seeds such as sunflower are considered a great source of protein, especially for vegetarians, as well as vitamin E (1 ounce contains 95 percent of the daily recommended value), among others. But remember, nuts and seeds can be high in fat and calories, so be mindful of portion sizes.

Three Bean Salad and More

This contemporary version of three-bean salad is a vast improvement over the canned version most of us ate as kids. It is an easy and wonderful dish to take to a picnic or potluck supper. The jalapeño pepper helps kick it up a notch, but if you prefer a less spicy version, feel free to leave it out.

Serves 4 as an entrée

1 pound green beans, trimmed

One 9-ounce package frozen lima beans

Cooked kernels from 2 ears corn (see page 50), or 2 cups frozen corn

One 15.5-ounce can red kidney beans, drained and rinsed

⅓ cup finely chopped celery

2 tablespoons chopped canned jalapeño chile peppers (wear plastic gloves when handling), optional

Spicy Vinaigrette (page 25)

8 cups bite-size pieces mixed greens

Olive oil, for drizzling

Bring 1" of water to a boil in the bottom of a steamer or saucepan. Put the green beans in the steamer basket, place over the boiling water, cover, and steam until crisp-tender, 6 to 7 minutes. Refresh under cold running water and drain. Add the lima beans, and frozen corn if using, to the basket, cover, and steam until thawed, about 2 minutes. Drain.

Combine the green beans, lima beans, fresh or thawed corn, kidney beans, celery, and jalapeños, if using, in a large bowl. Add the vinaigrette and toss to coat. Taste for seasoning.

Make a bed of lettuce on each of 4 plates. Spoon the salad on top and drizzle with any remaining vinaigrette. Finish each salad with a drizzle of olive oil and serve.

Per serving: 282 calories, 16 g protein, 57 g carbohydrates, 13 g total fat, 1 g saturated fat, 0 mg cholesterol, 19 g dietary fiber, 63 mg sodium

A WORD ABOUT WELLNESS

Studies have shown that losing even 5 to 10 percent of your body weight (that's just 10 to 20 pounds for a 200-pound person) can lower cholesterol and reduce your risks of high blood pressure and heart disease, diabetes, gall bladder disease, and some forms of cancer. Low-calorie foods and high-volume fruits and vegetables, which take up space and suppress appetite, can aid in any weight-loss program.

Mushroom-Zucchini Salad

This salad can be made with regular white mushrooms or the light brown cremini mushrooms, which have a deeper, woodsier flavor. Be sure to rinse the mushrooms quickly and pat dry with paper towels so they don't absorb water. For more protein, try adding sliced turkey. Feel free to use a bag of prepared mixed Italian lettuce in place of the arugula and radicchio.

Serves 4 as an entrée

½ pound white or cremini mushrooms, trimmed and sliced (about 4 cups)

½ pound (1 small) zucchini, trimmed, halved lengthwise, and sliced (about 2 cups)

¼ cup chopped red onion

One 15.5-ounce can cannellini beans, drained and rinsed

3 cups arugula

4 cups torn or sliced radicchio

Lemon-Oregano Dressing

1½ cups part-skim ricotta cheese

Combine the mushrooms, zucchini, onion, beans, arugula, and radicchio in a bowl. Add the dressing and toss. Divide the salad among 4 plates and add the ricotta by spoonfuls.

Per serving: 513 calories, 17 g protein, 25 g carbohydrates, 40 g total fat, 10 g saturated fat, 33 mg cholesterol, 5 g dietary fiber, 454 mg sodium

Lemon-Oregano Dressing

Serves 4

½ cup olive oil

3 tablespoons fresh lemon juice (from 1 lemon)

2 teaspoons chopped fresh oregano, or ½ teaspoon dried

1 clove garlic, minced

Salt and pepper to taste

Whisk together all of the ingredients in a small bowl until well combined.

Broccoli Salad with Tomatoes and Feta Cheese

This Greek-inspired salad is packed with tomato flavor. I like to use sun-dried tomatoes packed in oil because they're supple and ready to eat. If you prefer to use dried tomatoes, reconstitute them by soaking in boiling water for 1 minute.

Serves 4 as an entrée

1 head broccoli, trimmed and cut into florets

2 cups halved cherry tomatoes

2 cups sliced white mushrooms

16 black (Kalamata or other) olives, pitted if needed and halved

4 sun-dried tomatoes, chopped

1 shallot, thinly sliced

Salt and pepper to taste

Garlic-Balsamic Vinaigrette

8 cups bite-size pieces arugula, watercress, or romaine lettuce

¼ cup pine nuts or chopped pecans, toasted (see page 30)

4 ounces feta cheese, crumbled

Bring about 1" water to a boil in the bottom of a steamer or saucepan. Put the broccoli florets in the steamer basket, place over the boiling water, cover, and steam until the broccoli is just tender, 5 to 6 minutes. Drain in a colander, cool under cold, running water, and drain again.

In a large bowl, combine the broccoli, cherry tomatoes, mushrooms, olives, tomatoes, and shallot. Season with salt and pepper and toss. Add the dressing and toss again. Taste for seasoning.

Make a bed of greens on each of 4 plates. Spoon the salad on top, sprinkle with pine nuts or pecans and cheese and serve.

Per serving: *434 calories, 13 g protein, 23 g carbohydrates, 35 g total fat, 8 g saturated fat, 25 mg cholesterol, 7 g dietary fiber, 819 mg sodium*

Garlic-Balsamic Vinaigrette

Serves 4

½ cup olive oil

3 tablespoons balsamic vinegar

1 clove garlic, minced

Salt and pepper to taste

Whisk together all of the ingredients in a small bowl until well combined.

A WORD ABOUT WELLNESS

Lutein is an antioxidant found in broccoli that is important for vision and eye health, especially as we age. It may help prevent a condition called macular degeneration, which is a leading cause of blindness in older adults. However, because it is always present in our retinas, lutein may also help to improve our vision no matter what our age. Spinach, tomatoes, avocados, cabbage, red and orange bell peppers, peaches, and pears are just a few of the other lutein-rich foods we can reach for every day to ensure a brighter future.

Tortellini Salad

Unlike most tortellini salads, which offer little more than pasta, this one is loaded with fresh vegetables. Bocconcini are little balls of marinated mozzarella cheese. Many supermarkets carry them in the cured olive section or refrigerated section. You can pick up ½ pound of prepared bocconcini or make your own as directed below. Keep in mind that the cheese needs to marinate in the oil for at least an hour to absorb all of the flavor.

Serves 4 as an entrée

½ pound mozzarella, cut into cubes

¼ cup + 2 tablespoons olive oil

¼ teaspoon + ⅛ teaspoon red pepper flakes

¼ teaspoon minced garlic

Salt and pepper

3 ripe tomatoes, cut into ½" dice

1 large red bell pepper, seeded and cut into thin slices

3 ribs celery, sliced ¼" thick

½ cup chopped fresh parsley, or 1 tablespoon dried

½ cup slivered fresh basil, or 1 tablespoon dried

¼ teaspoon dried oregano

One 12-ounce package fresh cheese tortellini

¼ pound green beans, cut in half

8 cups arugula or spinach

To make the bocconcini, place the mozzarella cheese, ¼ cup of the olive oil, ¼ teaspoon of the red pepper flakes, the garlic, and salt and pepper to taste in a sealable container. Cover and refrigerate for 1 hour or up to 24 hours.

In a bowl, combine the tomatoes, bell pepper, celery, parsley, basil, oregano, remaining ⅛ teaspoon red pepper flakes, and salt to taste. Let stand for 1 hour.

Bring 3 quarts of salted water to a boil in a large saucepan. Add the tortellini and cook 3 minutes. Add the green beans and cook 3 minutes longer. Drain the pasta and beans, transfer to a bowl, and stir in the remaining 2 tablespoons oil to prevent the tortellini from sticking together. Let cool.

Add the tortellini and beans to the tomato mixture, along with the bocconcini and their flavored oil, and toss. Place the arugula on a serving platter, spoon the salad on top, and serve.

Per serving: 742 calories, 30 g protein, 56 g carbohydrates, 45 g total fat, 14 g saturated fat, 62 mg cholesterol, 8 g dietary fiber, 901 mg sodium

Mexican Brown Rice Salad

This is one of my favorite salads to bring to a potluck supper. It travels well and goes with any entrée. It can be served warm, at room temperature, or cold. If you're short on time you can use store-bought salsa instead of homemade.

Serves 4 as an entrée

5 tablespoons olive oil

½ cup diced onion

1 clove garlic, minced

¾ cup long-grain brown rice

Salt and pepper

1¾ cups water

1½ cups diced carrots (from 2 carrots)

¾ cup diced celery (from 2 ribs)

6 sprigs fresh parsley, or ½ teaspoon dried parsley

1 cup frozen green peas

One 15.5-ounce can pink beans, drained and rinsed

6–8 cups bite-size pieces romaine lettuce

1 tablespoon fresh lime juice

1 cup Fresh Tomato Salsa (page 105)

Heat 2 tablespoons olive oil in a large saucepan over medium-high heat. Add the onion and garlic and cook, stirring, until softened, about 2 minutes. Stir in the rice until well-coated with the oil, then season with salt and pepper to taste. Add the water and bring to a boil. Stir in the carrots, celery, and parsley. Reduce the heat to low, cover, and simmer until the rice is just tender, 30 to 40 minutes. Stir in the peas and beans, cover, and cook to warm through, 5 to 10 minutes longer. Remove from the heat. Discard the parsley sprigs, if using.

When ready to serve, toss the lettuce with the remaining olive oil, lime juice, and salt and pepper to taste. Divide among 4 plates. Spoon the rice on top of the greens, top with the salsa, and serve.

Per serving: 438 calories, 11 g protein, 57 g carbohydrates, 19 g total fat, 2 g saturated fat, 0 mg cholesterol, 11 g dietary fiber, 469 mg sodium

Wiley's Wisdom

Many different varieties of fresh produce contain an abundance of fiber, so salads are a great way to increase fiber intake. Given that most produce is naturally fat free, low in calories, and cholesterol free, a high-fiber diet incorporating these factors combats obesity and the many problems associated with being overweight.

Radicchio Salad with Chickpeas and Mango

If you're looking to add extra protein to this salad, try adding feta, Cheddar, or Monterey Jack cheese.

Serves 4 as an entrée

One 15.5-ounce can chickpeas, drained and rinsed

¼ cup chopped red onion

¼ cup roughly chopped fresh parsley, or 2 teaspoons dried

Bright Lemon Dressing (page 65)

4 cups sliced radicchio or red cabbage

4 cups bite-size pieces romaine lettuce

1 mango, diced (see page 53)

1 tomato, diced

1 cucumber, peeled and diced

1 green bell pepper, seeded and diced

One 8-ounce can water chestnuts, drained

Homemade Croutons (page 95), made with 4 slices whole wheat bread

Combine the chickpeas, onion, and parsley in a bowl and pour the dressing over. Use a fork to mash some of the chickpeas to allow the dressing to soak in. Let marinate while you prepare the rest of the vegetables.

Add the radicchio or cabbage, romaine lettuce, mango, tomato, cucumber, green pepper, water chestnuts, and croutons to the chickpea mixture. Toss until well combined and serve.

Per serving: 378 calories, 12 g protein, 51 g carbohydrates, 17 g total fat, 2 g saturated fat, 0 mg cholesterol, 14 g dietary fiber, 322 mg sodium

Stuffed Mushroom Salad

Stuffed mushrooms are traditionally served as hors d'oeuvres. Here they play the starring role atop a spinach-based salad.

Serves 4 as an entrée

¾ cup grated Parmesan cheese

⅓ cup fresh bread crumbs

¼ cup minced fresh parsley, or 2 teaspoons dried

3 scallions (white and green parts), thinly sliced

2 tablespoons low-fat plain yogurt, preferably Greek

4 tablespoons olive oil

Salt and pepper to taste

One 14-ounce package stuffing mushrooms (10 mushrooms), wiped clean and stems removed, or 4 portobello mushroom caps

2 slices turkey bacon (optional)

8 cups baby spinach

⅓ cup raisins

2 tablespoons balsamic vinegar

Preheat the oven to 400°F. Combine the cheese, bread crumbs, parsley, scallions, yogurt, and 2 tablespoons of the oil in a small bowl. Mix well and season with salt and pepper. Using a teaspoon, stuff the mushrooms with the mixture. Place the mushrooms on a rimmed baking sheet and bake until the topping is browned and crisp, about 20 minutes.

Meanwhile, if desired, cook the bacon in a skillet over medium heat, turning occasionally to brown evenly, 5 to 7 minutes. Drain on paper towels. When cool and crisp, crumble into small pieces.

Toss the spinach with the bacon if using, the raisins, vinegar, and remaining 2 tablespoons oil. Divide the salad among 4 plates, arrange 2 or 3 warm mushrooms on top of each, and serve.

Per serving: 289 calories, 12 g protein, 23 g carbohydrates, 18 g total fat, 5 g saturated fat, 14 mg cholesterol, 4 g dietary fiber, 418 mg sodium

Warm Kale Salad with White Beans and Corn

Kale with white beans is a traditional pairing found in Italian stews. Here the sautéed greens and cannellini beans are topped with creamy cottage cheese. If you like, frozen lima beans make a good substitute for the white beans. Cook them in boiling, salted water for 1 to 2 minutes, just until thawed.

Serves 4 as an entrée

5 tablespoons olive oil, plus more for serving

2 cloves garlic, thinly sliced

1 bunch (1½ pounds) kale, stemmed, leaves chopped

½ cup water

½ teaspoon dried oregano

Salt and pepper

One 15.5-ounce can cannellini beans, drained and rinsed

½ red onion, diced

1 red bell pepper, seeded and diced

1 cup grated carrot

10 black olives, pitted and halved

½ cup chopped fresh parsley, or 2 tablespoons dried

4 cups slivered romaine lettuce

Juice of ½ lemon

2 cups low-fat cottage cheese

⅓ cup sliced almonds

Cook 2 tablespoons of the oil and the garlic in a large pot over low heat until the garlic begins to turn golden brown. Add the kale, water, and oregano and season with salt. Cover and cook, stirring every now and then, for 10 minutes. Add the beans and onion and cook until the kale is tender but still has tooth, 15 to 25 minutes, depending on the age of the kale. Add more water if needed. Transfer to a large bowl and let cool 5 minutes.

Add the red pepper, carrot, olives, parsley, and remaining 3 tablespoons oil to the kale mixture. Toss and season with salt and pepper.

To serve, divide the lettuce among 4 bowls and top with the warm vegetables. Drizzle with the lemon juice and a little more oil. Place a scoop of cottage cheese on top of each serving, sprinkle with the almonds, and serve.

Per serving: 432 calories, 22 g protein, 45 g carbohydrates, 21 g total fat, 4 g saturated fat, 10 mg cholesterol, 9 g dietary fiber, 824 mg sodium

Roasted Fall Vegetable Salad

This delicious oven-baked salad sits on a lightly dressed bed of chicory—a bitter salad green. It's loaded with vegetable flavor, but if you want to add a bit of smokiness, crumble 4 slices of cooked turkey bacon on top.

Serves 4 as an entrée

1 pound Russet or Idaho potatoes, scrubbed and quartered

1 small (1½-pound) butternut squash, trimmed, peeled, and cut into ½" chunks (3 cups)

1 small onion, cut into 8 wedges

Salt and pepper to taste

6 tablespoons olive oil

¾ pound Brussels sprouts, halved if large

2 cups cherry tomatoes

7 cups chopped chicory leaves

3 tablespoons fresh lemon juice

Preheat the oven to 425°F. Spread the potatoes, squash, and onion in a single layer on a baking sheet. Season with salt and pepper and toss with 3 tablespoons of the oil until well coated. Roast 20 minutes.

Meanwhile, season the Brussels sprouts and tomatoes with salt and pepper in a bowl and toss with 1 tablespoon of the oil until well coated. Add to the pan after the other vegetables have roasted for 20 minutes. Continue roasting until all of the vegetables are nicely browned and tender when pierced with the tip of a small knife, about 15 minutes longer. Remove from the oven and cool slightly.

Toss the chicory leaves with the lemon juice and remaining 2 tablespoons oil. Season lightly with salt. Divide the chicory among 4 plates, top with the roasted vegetables, and serve.

Per serving: 447 calories, 12 g protein, 60 g carbohydrates, 22 g total fat, 3 g saturated fat, 0 mg cholesterol, 21 g dietary fiber, 241 mg sodium

A WORD ABOUT WELLNESS

Cooks have long known about the enhanced flavors and textures that result from slowly cooking down and reducing the amount of liquid in a dish. Good tasting becomes great tasting. What you may not have realized is that cooking some vegetables, such as carrots and tomatoes, actually breaks down their cell walls and frees up more nutrients—in these cases beta-carotene and lycopene—to be absorbed. Similarly, eating fruits such as raisins, dates, plums, blueberries, cranberries, and apricots that have been dried delivers a concentrated dose of their healthy charms.

Sweet Potato Pie Salad

Sweet potatoes are one of the most nostalgic vegetables from my childhood. Back when I was in college, my grandmother used to send me homemade sweet potato pies with a note saying, "Remember to share these with your friends." I was always the most popular guy in the dorm whenever those care packages arrived. This salad reminds me of those pies, with its sweet and savory flavors. I like using smaller sweet potatoes—they're likely to be sweeter. If you can't find collards, you can substitute kale or Swiss chard, cooked exactly the same way (but count on 5 to 10 minutes cooking time for the chard).

Serves 4 as an entrée

2 pounds small sweet potatoes

1 tablespoon olive oil

1 clove garlic, sliced

1 bunch (about 1 pound) collard greens, stems removed, leaves cut into 1" strips

½ cup water

Salt to taste

8 cups bite-size pieces mixed greens or one 12-ounce bag Veggie Lover's lettuce mix

Cooked kernels from 2 ears corn (see page 50), or 1½ cups frozen corn, thawed in the microwave 1 to 2 minutes

1 cup shredded Cheddar cheese or crumbled fresh goat cheese

2 scallions (green and white parts), thinly sliced

½ cup raisins

½ cup blueberries

½ cup pecans, toasted (see page 30) and chopped

Apple Cider Dressing (page 126)

Preheat the oven to 400°F. Prick the potatoes in several places with a fork. Place on a foil-lined baking sheet and roast until soft, 50 to 60 minutes. Let cool. Peel, cut in half lengthwise, and cut into large dice.

Cook the oil and garlic in a large, deep skillet (preferably nonstick) or large pot over medium-low heat until the garlic sizzles but does not brown, 1 to 2 minutes. Add the collards, water, and salt and stir. Cover and cook until the collards are tender but still chewy, 10 to 20 minutes, depending on the age of the collards. (If the water evaporates before the collards are cooked, add a little more.) Transfer to a bowl or plate to cool.

Combine the potatoes, collards, mixed greens, corn, cheese, scallions, raisins, blueberries, and pecans in a large bowl. Add the dressing, toss until well coated, and serve.

Per serving: 667 calories, 16 g protein, 57 g carbohydrates, 46 g total fat, 10 g saturated fat, 30 mg cholesterol, 12 g dietary fiber, 393 mg sodium

Blueberries are called "brain berries" or "youth berries" because lab studies have shown that their especially high levels of antioxidant phytochemicals may be able to, among other things, slow down or even reverse degenerative conditions such as dementia and Alzheimer's disease. In addition, one promising study showed that aging laboratory animals whose diet included the equivalent of 1 cup of blueberries a day actually demonstrated enhanced learning abilities, coordination, and balance. In other words, their brain age approximated that of a much younger animal. When compared with fruits and vegetables such as apples, carrots, broccoli, or squash, one serving of blueberries contains 5 servings' worth of the antioxidants of the other foods. Don't neglect these and other antioxidant-rich foods—simply remember blueberries when you think "brain food."

Warm Wild Rice Salad
with Swiss Chard, Broccoli, and Corn

There are a number of wild rice and brown rice mixes on the market now, including some with several different varieties of rice; use your favorite, or just substitute brown or wild rice. This salad also tastes great with sliced or diced banana. You can choose to omit the lettuces, in which case, add the olive oil to the salad along with the rice.

Serves 4 as an entrée

¾ cup wild and brown rice mix (or just brown rice or wild rice)

Salt and pepper

1 bunch (1–1½ pounds) Swiss chard or red chard

5 tablespoons olive oil

2 cloves garlic, sliced

¼ teaspoon dried red pepper flakes

1 large head broccoli, cut into florets

⅓ cup raisins

1 tablespoon red wine vinegar

Cooked kernels from 2 ears corn (see page 50), or 2 cups frozen corn, thawed in the microwave 1 to 2 minutes

¼ cup chopped red onion

1 carrot, grated

¼ cup fresh flat-leaf parsley leaves, chopped

6–8 cups thinly sliced romaine lettuce

Combine the rice mix, 1½ cups water, and salt to taste in a saucepan. Bring to a boil, reduce the heat to very low, cover, and simmer until the rice is tender and all the water has been absorbed, 40 to 45 minutes. Let stand, covered and off the heat, for 10 minutes.

Tear the chard leaves off the thick stems; reserve the stems. Wash the leaves and stems separately and drain. Tear the leaves into smallish pieces. Trim the stems and slice about ½" thick.

Cook 2 tablespoons of the oil and the garlic in a large skillet or pot over medium heat until the garlic begins to turn golden brown, 1 to 2 minutes. Add the red pepper flakes and stir. Add the chard stems and broccoli. Season with salt to taste and cook, stirring, 2 minutes. Add ½ cup water and increase the heat to high. Cover and cook, stirring every now and then, until the vegetables are just cooked through and the broccoli is still bright green, 5 to 6 minutes. Transfer to a bowl.

Add another tablespoon oil, the chard leaves, raisins, ¼ cup water, and salt to taste to the pan. Cover and cook over high heat, stirring every now and then, until the chard is limp, 4 to 5 minutes. Uncover, add the vinegar, and cook to evaporate the water and vinegar. Transfer to the bowl with the broccoli mixture. Let cool a few minutes. Add the corn, onion, carrot, and parsley.

Toss the romaine with the remaining 2 tablespoons oil. Add the rice and chard mixture and fold everything together. Season to taste with salt and pepper and serve.

Per serving: 469 calories, 14 g protein, 75 g carbohydrates, 17 g total fat, 2 g saturated fat, 0 mg cholesterol, 14 g dietary fiber, 515 mg sodium

A WORD ABOUT WELLNESS

Broccoli is number one on the National Cancer Institute's list of nutrition all-stars. In fact, broccoli (and other members of the cabbage family as well) tops the lists of experts everywhere as one of the foods most effective in fighting and preventing cancers. The primary reason appears to be broccoli's superior levels of phytochemicals called gluco-sinolates, which increase the body's antioxidant defense mechanisms and improve its ability to detoxify and eliminate harmful chemicals and hormones. Specifically, indoles appear to be especially beneficial to women in reducing risks of breast and cervical cancers. Studies show that isothiocyanates can help prevent lung and esophageal cancer as well as lowering the risks of cancers such as gastrointestinal. And these are only some of the cancer-fighting nutrients found in broccoli.

Grilled Sweet Potato and Eggplant Salad with Grapefruit and Chutney Dressing

Pink grapefruit is particularly nice in this salad because of its lovely color. The unique taste of grapefruit—not as sweet as orange, nor as tart as lemon or lime—not only complements the sweetness of the sweet potato, but brings out the flavor of the eggplant as well. Mango chutney (both mild and hot) for the dressing can be found in the ethnic (English) or specialty food aisles of most supermarkets.

Serves 4 as an entrée

1 small (about ½-pound) sweet potato, peeled and sliced into ½"-thick rounds

1 eggplant (¾–1 pound), trimmed but not peeled, cut into ½"-thick rounds

2 tablespoons olive or canola oil, for brushing

Salt and pepper to taste

2 teaspoons chili powder

1 pink or yellow grapefruit, peeled, sectioned, and coarsely chopped

½ cup chopped celery (from 2–3 ribs)

1 scallion (green and white parts), thinly sliced

Mango Chutney Dressing

8 cups bite-size pieces mixed greens or one 7-ounce bag Riviera lettuce mix

¾ cup diced Cheddar cheese

⅓ cup walnuts, toasted (see page 30) and chopped

Prepare a medium-hot grill or grill pan. Place the sweet potato and eggplant rounds on a baking sheet in a single layer. Brush with oil and sprinkle with salt and pepper. Working in batches, place the vegetables on the grill or pan, oiled side down. Brush the tops with oil and sprinkle with the chili powder and salt and pepper. Grill, turning once, until softened and well browned: 6 to 10 minutes for the eggplant and about 10 minutes for the sweet potato. Transfer the vegetables to a plate and cut the rounds in half. Let cool.

Transfer the vegetables to a bowl and add the grapefruit, celery, scallion, and half of the dressing. Toss gently.

Toss the greens with the remaining dressing. Divide among 4 plates. Spoon the vegetable mixture on top, sprinkle with the cheese and nuts, and serve.

Per serving: 532 calories, 11 g protein, 40 g carbohydrates, 38 g total fat, 8 g saturated fat, 23 mg cholesterol, 9 g dietary fiber, 409 mg sodium

Mango Chutney Dressing

Serves 4

⅓ cup olive oil

3 tablespoons fresh lime juice

2½ tablespoons store-bought mango chutney, chopped if necessary

Salt and pepper to taste

Whisk together all of the ingredients in a small bowl until well combined.

Winter Bread Salad

This dish is inspired by the Lebanese bread salad *fattoush*, made with pita bread. My version was developed for the winter months, when tomatoes are not in season but cherry tomatoes are available. Clementines add additional moisture and flavor and chickpeas add protein. If you make it in the summer, replace the cherry tomatoes with 3 cups cubed beefsteak tomatoes. And if you like, sprinkle ½ cup crumbled feta cheese or goat cheese, or shredded Cheddar cheese, over the top.

Serves 4 as an entrée

Two 7" whole wheat pita rounds

1 pint cherry tomatoes, each halved

Salt and pepper to taste

6 tablespoons olive oil, plus more for drizzling

½ cup chopped fresh parsley, or 2 tablespoons dried

One 15.5-ounce can chickpeas, drained and rinsed

3 clementines, peeled, sectioned, and roughly chopped

1 cucumber, peeled, quartered lengthwise, and chopped

1 red or green bell pepper, seeded and chopped

¼ cup low-fat plain yogurt, preferably Greek

½ cup orange juice

Juice of ½ lemon

½ teaspoon ground paprika

8 cups thinly sliced romaine lettuce

Preheat the oven to 375°F. Place the pitas on a baking sheet and bake until just crisp, 12 to 15 minutes. Let cool.

Meanwhile, place the cherry tomatoes in a bowl and season with salt. Add 3 tablespoons of the oil and the parsley. Crush the tomatoes with a wooden spoon to allow the salt to penetrate and release the juices. Set aside while you prepare everything else for the salad.

When the bread is cool, break it into pieces into the bowl with the tomatoes. Add the chickpeas, clementines, cucumber, and bell pepper and toss.

In a small bowl, whisk together the remaining 3 tablespoons oil, the yogurt, orange juice, lemon juice, paprika, and pepper. Pour over the salad and toss. Taste for salt and let stand for about an hour to allow the bread to soften.

Divide the lettuce among 4 plates and scoop the bread salad with its juices on top. Drizzle with additional olive oil and serve.

Per serving: 433 calories, 10 g protein, 52 g carbohydrates, 23 g total fat, 3 g saturated fat, 1 mg cholesterol, 11 g dietary fiber, 457 mg sodium

Spaghetti Squash Salad

This salad will help satisfy your pasta craving, without the carbs! When spaghetti squash cooks, the flesh breaks into strands, resembling spaghetti or angel hair pasta . . . thus the name. This is a wonderful salad for kids, especially those who might not otherwise like eating vegetables!

Serves 4 as an entrée

1 spaghetti squash (1½–2 pounds), halved and seeded

1 tablespoon olive oil

Salt to taste

4 cups baby spinach

1 large red bell pepper, seeded and cut into strips

1 cup frozen peas

5 tablespoons grated Parmesan cheese

Lemon-Basil Dressing

8 cups bite-size soft lettuces, such as Boston or red leaf, or 2 bags Sweet Butter lettuce

Preheat the oven to 350°F. Drizzle the cut sides of the squash with the oil and sprinkle with salt. Place cut-side down on a baking sheet. Roast until the squash is tender when pierced (through the peel) with a small knife, about 40 minutes. Let cool.

Scoop out the squash in strands with either a spoon or a fork and transfer to a bowl. Add the spinach, red pepper, peas, Parmesan, and dressing and toss.

Divide the lettuce among 4 plates or shallow bowls. Spoon the squash mixture over and serve.

Per serving: 357 calories, 8 g protein, 25 g carbohydrates, 27 g total fat, 4 g saturated fat, 6 mg cholesterol, 5 g dietary fiber, 360 mg sodium

Lemon-Basil Dressing

Serves 4

6 tablespoons olive oil

2 tablespoons fresh lemon juice

2 tablespoons chopped basil, or 1 teaspoon dried

1 tablespoon water

¼ teaspoon crushed red pepper flakes

Salt and pepper to taste

Whisk together all of the ingredients in a small bowl until well combined.

Mashed Potato Salad

The comic strip character Dagwood always took mashed potato sandwiches to work. I'm sure he would have loved this salad, if he only knew about it! Creamy mashed potatoes taste great with bitter vegetables such as broccoli rabe and bitter greens like escarole, radicchio, and endive. You can use any variety of potato here—Idahos give a fluffy-textured mashed potato, while new potatoes and Yukon Golds are finer textured and more dense. Black or green olives are tasty in this, too.

Serves 4 as an entrée

1½ pounds Idaho or russet potatoes, peeled and cubed (about 4 cups)

Salt and pepper to taste

1 bunch broccoli rabe, trimmed and cut crosswise into thirds, or 1 head broccoli, trimmed

2 tablespoons olive oil

2 cloves garlic, sliced

½ cup buttermilk

2 tablespoons chopped chives or scallion greens

8 cups bite-size pieces hardy, bitter greens such as escarole, radicchio, or endive

1 cup frozen green peas, thawed in the microwave

1 green or red bell pepper, seeded and chopped

Cooked kernels from 2 ears corn (see page 50), or 2 cups frozen corn, thawed in the microwave 1 to 2 minutes

Spicy Vinaigrette (page 25)

1 cup shredded Cheddar cheese

In a saucepan, combine the potatoes and salted water to cover. Bring to a boil, reduce to a simmer, and cook until the potatoes are tender when pierced with the tip of a small knife, about 15 minutes.

Place the broccoli rabe in a bowl, add water to cover, and swish in the water to rinse. Lift the broccoli rabe out of the bowl and drain in a colander.

Cook the oil and garlic in a large saucepan over medium-low heat until the garlic sizzles and just begins to brown, 1 to 2 minutes. Add the broccoli rabe and sprinkle with salt. Cover and cook until the broccoli rabe is tender when you squeeze it between two fingers, about 5 minutes. Uncover and cook until all of the water evaporates. Remove from the heat and set aside.

When the potatoes are cooked, drain in a colander. Transfer to a bowl and mash with a potato masher. Stir in the buttermilk and chives or scallion and season with salt and pepper.

Toss together the greens, peas, bell pepper, corn, and vinaigrette. Divide among 4 plates. Spoon the broccoli rabe on top, and then the mashed potatoes. Sprinkle with the cheese and serve.

Per serving: 612 calories, 19 g protein, 61 g carbohydrates, 36 g total fat, 10 g saturated fat, 31 mg cholesterol, 9 g dietary fiber, 370 mg sodium

Roasted Winter Vegetable Salad

Roasting vegetables allows for further development of their flavors. Here they are simply spread out on a baking sheet, coated with a balsamic vinaigrette, and roasted at high heat for a bit. The result is a delicious, rich, caramelized taste. This salad uses many of my favorite root vegetables including beets, carrots, parsnips, and rutabaga. Serve it warm or at room temperature.

Serves 4 as an entrée

1 bunch (about ¾ pound) small beets, trimmed, peeled, and cut into 1" cubes

2 carrots, peeled and cut into 1" chunks (about 2 cups)

2 parsnips, peeled and cut into 1" chunks (about 2 cups)

2 turnips, peeled and cut into 1" chunks (about 2 cups)

½ rutabaga, peeled and cut into 1" chunks (about 2 cups)

1 small red onion, cut into 1" dice

2 Granny Smith apples, peeled, cored, and cut into 1" dice

9 tablespoons canola or olive oil

4 tablespoons balsamic vinegar

Salt and pepper to taste

2 tablespoons chopped fresh parsley

8 cups arugula, watercress, or bite-size pieces romaine lettuce, or one 9-ounce bag Italian lettuce mix

Preheat the oven to 375°F. In a bowl, toss the beets, carrots, parsnips, turnips, rutabaga, onion, and apples with 6 tablespoons of the oil, 3 tablespoons of the vinegar, and salt and pepper. Spread out on a sheet pan or in a shallow baking dish in a single layer (if you have too many vegetables, divide between 2 pans). Roast, stirring from time to time, until tender but still firm and nicely browned, about 30 minutes. Stir in the parsley and set aside.

Whisk together the remaining 1 tablespoon vinegar and 3 tablespoons oil in a large bowl. Season with salt and pepper. Add the lettuce and toss. Divide the lettuce among 4 plates, spoon the vegetables on top, and serve.

Per serving: 474 calories, 5 g protein, 46 g carbohydrates, 32 g total fat, 2 g saturated fat, 0 mg cholesterol, 12 g dietary fiber, 208 mg sodium

Red Cabbage Salad with Sesame Dressing

Even though we think about leafy greens being green in color, there are plenty of "greens" that are actually red, such as cabbage and red leaf lettuce. Red cabbage makes a beautiful presentation here. It pairs nicely with the citrus and sesame flavors in the salad. If you prefer poultry in your entrée salad, ½ pound of sliced deli turkey makes a convenient addition to this dish.

Serves 4 as an entrée

4 cups thinly sliced red cabbage

1 zucchini, cut on an angle into ¼"-thick slices

1 navel orange, peeled and cut into ½" cubes

Sesame Dressing

Combine the cabbage, zucchini, and orange in a bowl. Pour the dressing over, toss until well combined, and serve.

Per serving: 180 calories, 3 g protein, 15 g carbohydrates, 14 g total fat, 2 g saturated fat, 0 mg cholesterol, 3 g dietary fiber, 560 mg sodium

Sesame Dressing

Serves 4

¼ cup reduced-sodium soy sauce

¼ cup Asian toasted sesame oil

2 teaspoons sugar

Whisk together all of the ingredients in a small bowl until well combined.

Roasted Cauliflower Salad with Curry Dressing

I used to always think of cauliflower as a bland, boring vegetable. This appealing fall salad changed all that, combining the sweet, savory, and tart flavors of cauliflower and apples. Roasting the cauliflower helps caramelize it, bringing out its rich, nutty flavor.

Serves 4 as an entrée

1 head cauliflower, cored and cut into bite-size florets

Salt and pepper to taste

1 tablespoon olive oil

1 Granny Smith apple, cored and cut into bite-size chunks

1½ cups halved seedless red or green grapes

½ cup sliced (on the bias) celery

3 scallions (green and white parts), thinly sliced

3 tablespoons golden raisins

One 15.5-ounce can chickpeas, drained and rinsed

Curry Dressing (page 74)

¼ cup sliced almonds

3 tablespoons chopped fresh cilantro

8 cups baby spinach

Preheat the oven to 450°F. Place the cauliflower florets in a roasting pan large enough to hold them in a single layer. Sprinkle with salt and pepper, drizzle with the oil, and toss to coat. Roast, stirring every 5 minutes, until the cauliflower is tender and lightly browned, about 15 minutes. Let cool.

Transfer the roasted cauliflower to a large bowl. Add the apple, grapes, celery, scallions, raisins, and chickpeas. Pour the dressing over and toss. Sprinkle with the almonds and cilantro.

Make a bed of spinach leaves on a platter or 4 serving plates. Spoon the salad on top and serve.

Per serving: 301 calories, 10 g protein, 54 g carbohydrates, 8 g total fat, 1 g saturated fat, 0 mg cholesterol, 12 g dietary fiber, 444 mg sodium

Kale and Brown Rice Salad

Kale is often relegated to the role of garnish on plates or at salad bars, rather than the main attraction of a meal. Here it stars in its own right! You can make this salad with a variety of greens, such as kale, collards, greens, or Swiss chard, or a combination of different greens. If using a combination, start longer-cooking greens (kale) first, and then add the shorter-cooking greens later. Kale takes 15 to 20 minutes to cook, collards 10 to 15 minutes, and Swiss chard 5 to 10 minutes. Swiss chard stems taste good, too; cut them into 1" lengths and cook along with the greens, about 15 minutes.

Serves 4 as an entrée

¾ cup brown rice

Salt and pepper to taste

2 tablespoons olive oil

1¾–2 pounds kale, stemmed, rinsed well, leaves cut crosswise into 1"-wide strips

2 cloves garlic, sliced

⅛ teaspoon dried red pepper flakes

½ pound shiitake mushrooms, stemmed and cut in half

1 red bell pepper, seeded and cut into strips

One 8-ounce can water chestnuts, drained

2 tablespoons seasoned rice wine vinegar

2 scallions (white and green parts), thinly sliced

2 teaspoons Asian toasted sesame oil

8 cups mixed greens

Combine the rice, 1¾ cups water, and ¾ teaspoon salt in a saucepan. Bring to a boil and reduce the heat to very low. Cover and simmer until the rice is tender and all the water has been absorbed, about 40 minutes.

Heat 1 tablespoon of the olive oil in a large skillet over medium heat. Add the kale, ½ cup water, and salt to taste. Cover and cook, stirring occasionally, until the kale is tender but still chewy, 15 to 20 minutes. Transfer to a bowl.

Add the remaining 1 tablespoon olive oil, the garlic, and red pepper flakes to the pan. Cook over medium-low heat until the garlic sizzles but does not brown, 1 to 2 minutes. Add the mushrooms, bell pepper, water chestnuts, and salt to taste. Increase the heat to medium-high and cook, stirring, 2 minutes. Add the vinegar and cook, stirring, until evaporated. Return the kale to the pan, turn off the heat, and stir to combine. Let cool a few minutes.

In a large bowl, stir together the rice, kale mixture, scallions, sesame oil, and salt and pepper to taste. Divide the greens among 4 plates, spoon the salad over, and serve.

Per serving: 400 calories, 13 g protein, 68 g carbohydrates, 12 g total fat, 2 g saturated fat, 0 mg cholesterol, 13 g dietary fiber, 198 mg sodium

Freezer Vegetable Salad

In this salad the vegetables, all easily found in the freezer section of your grocery store, are tossed with cheese while still warm, causing the cheese to melt into a luscious texture. Use low-fat or full-fat cheese (not fat-free) in this recipe. Before going out to the store to buy the ingredients for this salad, be sure to check your freezer—you probably have many of them on hand already!

Serves 4 as an entrée

Salt to taste

½ (10-ounce) package frozen lima beans

½ (9-ounce) package frozen string beans

½ (10-ounce) package frozen green peas

½ (10-ounce) package frozen corn kernels

1 cup shredded pepper Jack cheese (about 3 ounces)

Apple Cider Dressing (page 126)

½ cup apple juice

One 16-ounce bag prepared coleslaw mix, or broccoli slaw mix

Bring 1 cup of salted water to a boil in a small saucepan. Add the lima beans, cover, and cook 2 minutes. Add the rest of the vegetables and cook, covered, 5 more minutes, stirring every now and then for even cooking. Drain, and transfer to a bowl. Add the cheese while the vegetables are still warm. Add the dressing and the apple juice, toss, and let the vegetables stand for a few minutes to cool to room temperature.

To serve, add the cabbage and toss.

Per serving: 433 calories, 12 g protein, 37 g carbohydrates, 28 g total fat, 6 g saturated fat, 19 mg cholesterol, 8 g dietary fiber, 373 mg sodium

Russian Potato Salad

Deep pink in color, I call this salad "Russian" because of the delicious addition of beets. The recipe is a snap to make if you buy beets that are already cooked—either jarred, or in packages in the produce aisle of your supermarket. Let the salad sit for a few hours in the refrigerator to let the flavors develop.

Serves 4 as an entrée

1 pound new or small Yukon gold potatoes

1½ cups ¾"-cubed roasted beets (see page 33)

4 hard-cooked eggs, cut into ½" dice

6 small ribs celery, chopped

1 cup frozen peas, heated in the microwave 1 to 2 minutes until thawed

¼ cup diced dill pickles

2 tablespoons minced red onion

Dill Dressing

8 cups bite-size pieces mixed greens

Place the potatoes, whole and unpeeled, in a saucepan and add cold water to cover. Bring to a boil, reduce the heat, and simmer until tender when pierced with the tip of a small knife, 20 to 25 minutes. Let cool. Peel and cut into ¾" cubes.

In bowl, toss together the potatoes, beets, eggs, celery, peas, pickles, onion, and dressing. Cover and refrigerate for 2 hours to let the flavors develop.

Make a bed of lettuce on each of 4 plates, spoon the salad on top, and serve.

Per serving: *403 calories, 13 g protein, 30 g carbohydrates, 26 g total fat, 5 g saturated fat, 212 mg cholesterol, 8 g dietary fiber, 845 mg sodium*

Dill Dressing

Serves 4

6 tablespoons olive oil

¼ cup apple cider vinegar

¼ cup chopped fresh dill, or 2 teaspoons dried

2 tablespoons Dijon mustard

Salt and pepper to taste

Whisk together all of the ingredients in a small bowl until well combined.

Chapter 6

Side Salads

S ide salads make the perfect accompaniment to a main course, whether it is grilled or roasted chicken or fish, or an entrée salad. Side salads should be presented in a separate bowl or platter, or served on salad plates, placed to the left of the dinner plate. If pasta, rice, or potatoes are served as sides, I suggest that the salad not be placed on the same plate. Side salads should always be interesting, attractive, and appetizing; however, they should not be the stars of the show when served during the main course. So while it's okay to have a colorful side salad like Green Apple and Pea Salad with Lemon-Horseradish Dressing (page 182), a side salad is primarily for balance and for additional fruit and vegetable servings. Remember these tips when determining your selection.

- The side salad isn't a stand-alone dish. It's served to complement the meal. In most cases, it's served in place of a standard cooked vegetable or fruit side dish.

- Sides shouldn't be too sweet or too tart. They should go with your main course. If you are serving a nonmeat or nonfish meal, then this salad should complement the other sides and should never outperform them.

- Consider serving a side salad in small individual bowls so that the flavor remains distinct and doesn't compete with other items on the entrée plate.

- Many of these salads can alternately be served as a starter salad or first course.

Side Salads

*Salad Man Selects recipes

Corn and Black Bean Salad with Pepper-Lime Dressing

This easy side salad also makes a wonderful relish or topping for grilled chicken, meat, or fish.

Serves 4 as a side

Cooked kernels from 2 ears corn (see page 50), or 2 cups frozen corn, thawed in the microwave 1 to 2 minutes

One 15.5-ounce can black beans, drained and rinsed

½ cup diced red bell pepper

½ cup diced green bell pepper

½ red onion, diced

Pepper-Lime Dressing

4 cups red leaf lettuce

Combine the corn, beans, red pepper, green pepper, onion, and dressing in a large bowl and gently toss until well combined. Divide the lettuce among 5 individual bowls and top with the salad.

Per serving: *325 calories, 8 g protein, 35 g carbohydrates, 20 g total fat, 3 g saturated fat, 0 mg cholesterol, 8 g dietary fiber, 360 mg sodium*

Pepper-Lime Dressing

Serves 4

⅓ cup olive oil

Juice of 1 lime

1 jalapeño chile pepper, cored, seeded, and chopped (wear plastic gloves when handling)

Salt and pepper to taste

Whisk together all of the ingredients in a small bowl until well combined.

A WORD ABOUT WELLNESS

Beans—including lentils, black beans, pinto beans, kidney beans, and chickpeas—may be the darlings of dietary fiber. While many cooked vegetables supply only 2 to 3 grams of fiber per ½ cup, that amount of beans supplies about 8 grams. Fiber is believed to help keep "bad" cholesterol numbers down and to elevate the "good," to normalize blood sugar levels and so reduce the risk of developing type 2 diabetes, and to facilitate weight loss.

Succotash Salad with Citrus Vinaigrette

This traditional Southern dish is an homage to summer, when corn, tomatoes, and beans are at the peak of ripeness. The vegetables are tossed here in a light, simple vinaigrette that allows their full flavors to come through.

Serves 4 as a side

2 cups frozen lima beans

1 cup frozen peas

Cooked kernels from 2 ears corn (see page 50), or 2 cups frozen corn, thawed in the microwave 1 to 2 minutes

1 tomato, diced

2 scallions (green and white parts), diced

Citrus Vinaigrette

Blanch the lima beans and peas in boiling water for 4 minutes. Drain and rinse under cold running water to end the cooking process. Let the vegetables drain thoroughly.

In a large bowl, combine the lima beans, peas, corn, tomato, scallions, and vinaigrette. Toss gently and serve.

Per serving: 350 calories, 9 g protein, 40 g carbohydrates, 19 g total fat, 3 g saturated fat, 0 mg cholesterol, 8 g dietary fiber, 249 mg sodium

Citrus Vinaigrette

Serves 4

⅓ cup olive oil

2 tablespoons lemon juice

1 tablespoon red wine vinegar

Salt and pepper to taste

Whisk together all of the ingredients in a small bowl until well combined.

Garden Pasta Salad

This pasta salad is great for kids because the noodles are the star attraction, even though it's packed with vegetables. Feel free to add any of your favorites such as asparagus, yellow squash, or sugar snap peas. For an alternative to raw vegetables, try grilling the zucchini, peppers, and onion before adding them to the salad.

Serves 4 as a side

8 ounces pasta shells

1 tablespoon vegetable oil

3 tablespoons olive oil

3 tablespoons red wine vinegar

1 tablespoon lime juice

1 tablespoon sugar

1 tablespoon finely chopped fresh basil

1 clove garlic, minced

1 cup chopped tomato

½ cup cubed seeded cucumber

½ cup sliced halved zucchini

½ cup shredded red cabbage

½ red bell pepper, seeded and julienned

½ orange or yellow bell pepper, seeded and julienned

1 tablespoon diced onion

Salt and pepper to taste

Cook the pasta in a large pot of boiling water according to the package directions. Drain and rinse under cold running water. Place the pasta in a large bowl, add the vegetable oil, and mix. Refrigerate until ready to use.

In a small bowl, combine the olive oil, vinegar, lime juice, sugar, basil, and garlic and whisk until blended.

Add the tomato, cucumber, zucchini, cabbage, red pepper, orange or yellow pepper, and onion to the pasta and toss to mix. Add the dressing and salt and pepper, toss again, and serve.

Per serving: 369 calories, 9 g protein, 51 g carbohydrates, 15 g total fat, 2 g saturated fat, 0 mg cholesterol, 3 g dietary fiber, 84 mg sodium

Chow-Chow Salad

When I was growing up, tomatoes and cabbage were always in abundance. They were the main ingredients in my favorite relish, chow-chow pickles (pronounced *cha-cha*). This delish relish can be served to enhance black-eyed peas, beans, or collards. If you're looking to save some time, substitute a bag of pre-shredded cabbage and carrots for the cabbage and carrots in the recipe.

Serves 4 as a side

4 cups shredded green cabbage

2 carrots, shredded

1 cucumber, peeled and sliced

1 green bell pepper, seeded and diced

6 tablespoons white wine vinegar

¼ cup sugar

¼ cup canola oil

2 tablespoons water

Salt to taste (I recommend 2 teaspoons for pickling)

Combine all of the ingredients in a bowl, cover, and marinate at least 2 hours or overnight before serving.

Per serving: 214 calories, 2 g protein, 22 g carbohydrates, 15 g total fat, 1 g saturated fat, 0 mg cholesterol, 4 g dietary fiber, 1,199 mg sodium

Green Bean, Corn, and Tomato Salad

The beauty of this simple salad lies in its versatility. You can add or swap out any other summer vegetables including zucchini, summer squash, and peas.

Serves 4 as a side

1 pound green beans, trimmed

3 cups salad greens

2 tomatoes, peeled, seeded, and diced

Cooked kernels from 1 ear corn (see page 50), or 1 cup frozen corn, thawed in the microwave 1 to 2 minutes

Basil-Garlic Vinaigrette

Bring about 1 inch water to a boil in the bottom of a steamer or saucepan. Put the green beans in the steamer basket, place over the boiling water, cover, and steam until tender, about 5 minutes. Rinse the beans under cold running water to stop the cooking process. Pat dry with paper towels.

Combine the beans, greens, tomatoes, corn, and dressing in a large bowl and gently toss until well combined. Let sit for 1 to 2 hours before serving.

Per serving: 244 calories, 4 g protein, 20 g carbohydrates, 19 g total fat, 3 g saturated fat, 0 mg cholesterol, 7 g dietary fiber, 16 mg sodium

Basil-Garlic Vinaigrette

Serves 4

⅓ cup olive oil

2 tablespoons red wine vinegar

6 fresh basil leaves, minced

1 clove garlic, minced

Whisk together all of the ingredients in a small bowl until well combined.

Easy Tabbouleh Salad

Bulgur wheat is a quick-cooking form of whole wheat. It is similar to cracked wheat, and is used like couscous and rice. Try serving this traditional Middle Eastern salad wrapped in lettuce leaves alongside grilled chicken or meat.

Serves 4 as a side

6 ounces finely ground bulgur wheat

1½ cups warm water

Juice of 1 lemon

⅓ cup olive oil

Pinch turmeric

Salt and pepper to taste

1 pound tomatoes, halved, seeded, and cubed

3 scallions (green and white parts), chopped

1 large cucumber, seeded and diced

2 tablespoons finely chopped fresh mint

3 tablespoons finely chopped fresh parsley

Place the bulgur in a bowl and add the warm water. Let sit for at least 1 hour or until all the water is absorbed and the bulgur is tender. Add more water if needed.

In a small bowl, whisk together the lemon juice, oil, turmeric, and salt and pepper until well blended. Set aside.

In a large bowl, combine the bulgur, tomatoes, scallions, cucumber, mint, and parsley. Add the dressing and gently toss until well combined. Let the salad sit for 20 minutes before serving.

Per serving: *342 calories, 7 g protein, 40 g carbohydrates, 19 g total fat, 3 g saturated fat, 0 mg cholesterol, 10 g dietary fiber, 95 mg sodium*

Cucumber-Yogurt Salad

Try serving this salad in little vegetable "boats," such as hollowed-out tomatoes, halved and seeded bell peppers, endive spears, or celery stalks. For an even easier preparation, pulse the cucumber in the food processor to chop.

Serves 4 as a side

2 cucumbers, peeled and diced

Salt to taste

2 cups low-fat plain yogurt, preferably Greek

2 tablespoons olive oil

¼ cup fresh dill or mint, finely chopped, or 2 teaspoons dried

2 teaspoons crushed garlic

½ teaspoon pepper

Place the diced cucumbers in a colander, sprinkle with salt, and let drain for about 15 minutes. Rinse quickly under cold running water. Press down on the cucumbers in the colander to remove any excess liquid. Dry with paper towels.

In a large bowl, combine the cucumbers, yogurt, oil, dill or mint, garlic, and pepper. Stir to combine. Taste for salt, although you probably won't need to add more.

Per serving: *158 calories, 7 g protein, 12 g carbohydrates, 9 g total fat, 2 g saturated fat, 7 mg cholesterol, 1 g dietary fiber, 161 mg sodium*

Zucchini Salad with Garlic and Tomatoes

This salad is simple, delicious, and an unusual presentation for zucchini. It makes a wonderful addition to any buffet table.

Serves 4 as a side

¼ cup olive oil, plus more for serving

1 pound zucchini, sliced ¼" thick

2 tablespoons chopped fresh parsley

1 clove garlic, chopped

Salt and pepper to taste

1½ envelopes unflavored gelatin

⅓ cup water

1 cup low-sodium chicken broth

2 large beefsteak tomatoes

Heat the oil in a large skillet over medium-high heat. Add the zucchini and cook, stirring every now and then, 5 minutes. Add the parsley and garlic and continue cooking until the zucchini is just tender but still bright green, about 5 minutes longer. Season with salt and pepper. Transfer to a food processor and process to small pieces.

Sprinkle the gelatin over the water in a large bowl and let stand 2 minutes. Heat the broth in a saucepan over medium heat until warm. Pour the broth over the gelatin and stir to dissolve. Stir in the zucchini. Pour into a 9×5" bread pan that has been lined with plastic wrap. Cover with plastic and refrigerate several hours, until set.

To serve, turn the mold out onto a platter. Slice the tomatoes, arrange on a plate, and drizzle with a little olive oil. Sprinkle with salt. Slice the mold and serve with the tomatoes.

Per serving: 175 calories, 6 g protein, 8 g carbohydrates, 14 g total fat, 2 g saturated fat, 6 mg cholesterol, 3 g dietary fiber, 205 mg sodium

Sugar Snap Pea Salad with Corn and Cherry Tomatoes

Some of my all-time favorite flavors of summer are combined in this tangy salad. I've added blueberries because they pair so well with the tanginess of the Blue Cheese–Buttermilk Dressing.

Serves 4 as a side

¾ pound sugar snap peas

4 cups watercress, arugula, spinach, or bite-size pieces romaine lettuce

Cooked kernels from 1 ear corn (see page 50), or 1 cup frozen corn, thawed in the microwave 1 to 2 minutes

1 cup blueberries

1 cup halved cherry tomatoes

Blue Cheese–Buttermilk Dressing (page 40)

2 scallions (green and white parts), chopped

Bring a saucepan of salted water to a boil. Add the peas and cook until barely tender, about 1 minute. Drain and rinse under cold running water to stop the cooking. Drain.

Toss the peas, greens, corn, blueberries, and tomatoes in a serving bowl. Drizzle the dressing over, sprinkle with the scallions, and serve.

Per serving: 574 calories, 18 g protein, 32 g carbohydrates, 42 g total fat, 13 g saturated fat, 63 mg cholesterol, 5 g dietary fiber, 1,353 mg sodium

Wiley's Wisdom

Watercress is a wonderfully delicious and versatile salad green, but it shouldn't be handled or stored like other salad greens. Given its delicate nature, watercress leaves should be washed and completely dried with paper towels, then loosely placed in a glass jar. Tighten the jar lid and refrigerate. Stored this way, watercress will remain fresh for 3 to 5 days.

Southern Potato Salad

In the South, everyone I know has their favorite version of potato salad that they make for Sunday dinner and throughout the week. This recipe is the updated, lower fat version of my favorite one from childhood. A bit of reduced-fat sour cream helps add a creamy touch.

Serves 4 as a side

2 pounds new potatoes, peeled and cut into ¾" cubes

⅓ cup reduced-fat mayonnaise

⅓ cup reduced-fat sour cream

2 tablespoons white vinegar

1½ tablespoons whole grain mustard

1 tablespoon celery seed (optional)

Salt and pepper to taste

¾ cup chopped celery

½ cup jarred pimientos, finely diced

¼ cup chopped onion

2 hard-cooked eggs, chopped

Cover the potatoes with cold water in a saucepan, bring to a simmer, and cook until almost tender, 6 to 8 minutes.

Meanwhile, in a medium mixing bowl, combine the mayonnaise, sour cream, vinegar, mustard, and celery seed. Season with salt and pepper.

When the potatoes are cooked, drain, and while still warm, add to the bowl with the dressing; toss. Let cool to room temperature.

Add the celery, pimientos, onion, and eggs to the potato mixture, toss until well combined, and serve.

Per serving: 174 calories, 9 g protein, 17 g carbohydrates, 8 g total fat, 3 g saturated fat, 114 mg cholesterol, 7 g dietary fiber, 395 mg sodium

Brown Rice Salad with Feta Cheese

The zest from lemon gives this colorful salad a bright, clean flavor. For variety, try using lime and basil instead of lemon and parsley.

Serves 4 as a side

½ cup brown rice

1 cup water

1 lemon

3 tablespoons olive oil

Salt and pepper to taste

2 cups cherry tomatoes, each halved

Cooked kernels from 1 ear corn (see page 50), or 1 cup frozen corn, thawed in the microwave 1 to 2 minutes

1 cup chopped scallions (green and white parts)

1 cup chopped fresh parsley, or 1 tablespoon dried

4 cups baby arugula

½ cup crumbled feta or goat cheese

Combine the rice and water in a small saucepan. Bring to a boil over high heat, reduce the heat, cover, and simmer until tender, 30 to 40 minutes. Let stand off heat for 10 minutes. Transfer to a large mixing bowl and let cool to room temperature. Grate the lemon zest directly over the rice.

Halve the lemon and squeeze the juice into a small mixing bowl. Add the oil and salt and pepper and whisk to combine.

Add the tomatoes, corn, scallions, parsley, and half the dressing to the rice and toss well. Toss the arugula with the remaining dressing in a separate bowl.

Divide the arugula among 4 plates. Top with the rice mixture, sprinkle with the cheese, and serve.

Per serving: 288 calories, 8 g protein, 33 g carbohydrates, 16 g total fat, 4 g saturated fat, 17 mg cholesterol, 5 g dietary fiber, 309 mg sodium

Pool Room Slaw

I like to make this salad with whatever I have on hand in the refrigerator. Also try adding cooked lima beans, grated raw beet, grated sweet potato, cooked sweet potato, red or green bell pepper, scallions, raw spinach, other lettuces, or olives.

Serves 4 as a side

2 cups slivered red cabbage

2 cups slivered green cabbage

½ cucumber, peeled, cut in half lengthwise, seeded, and sliced

1 carrot, grated

½ Granny Smith apple, cored and sliced

7 radishes, sliced

⅓ cup chopped fresh parsley, or 1 tablespoon dried

⅓ cup pecans, toasted (see page 30) and chopped

¼ cup chopped red onion

Lemon-Honey Dressing (page 36)

1 banana

In a large bowl, combine the red cabbage, green cabbage, cucumber, carrot, apple, radishes, parsley, pecans, onion, and dressing and toss. Peel and slice the banana and add to the salad just before serving so that it doesn't brown or get soft.

Per serving: 314 calories, 3 g protein, 25 g carbohydrates, 24 g total fat, 3 g saturated fat, 0 mg cholesterol, 5 g dietary fiber, 114 mg sodium

Roasted Peppers with Garlic Dressing

This salad reminds me of the peppers we used to plant in pots on the front porch of our house in Alabama. They were as beautiful to look at as they were to eat! Find a sunny spot and plant your own! Roasting helps sweeten the flesh of bell peppers. You can use any color, but red and yellow are the tastiest. Steaming the peppers in a bowl after roasting makes removing the skin easy. Since there are so few ingredients in this salad, try and roast fresh peppers, if possible.

Serves 4 as a side

4 bell peppers, roasted, or four 7½-ounce jars roasted peppers (each jar contains 1 pepper)

Garlic-Balsamic Vinaigrette (page 145)

4 red leaf lettuce leaves

2 scallions (white and green parts), thinly sliced

Slice the peppers into 1½-inch-thick slices. Place in a bowl and pour the vinaigrette over. Place the lettuce leaves on a serving platter. Place the peppers on top of the lettuce leaves, sprinkle with the scallions, and serve immediately. Or, if you prefer, let the peppers marinate for several hours to absorb the flavors of the vinaigrette before serving on top of the lettuce leaves.

Per serving: *446 calories, 2 g protein, 12 g carbohydrates, 54 g total fat, 7 g saturated fat, 0 mg cholesterol, 2 g dietary fiber, 592 mg sodium*

Roasting Peppers

Preheat the oven to 500°F. Place fresh peppers on a baking sheet and roast, turning every now and then, until they soften and the skins shrivel, 10 to 15 minutes. Transfer the peppers to a bowl, cover with plastic wrap, and set aside until cool. Pull off the stems, scrape out the seeds with your fingers, and peel off the skins.

Green Apple and Pea Salad with Lemon-Horseradish Dressing

This salad is so very versatile! Not only is it perfect as a side dish, it can also become a first course when placed on a bed of winter greens, or an entrée salad when served topped with grilled chicken.

Serves 4 as a side

2 cups frozen green peas

1 cup cherry tomatoes, each halved

1 Granny Smith apple, cored and cubed

4 scallions (green and white parts), chopped

Lemon-Horseradish Dressing

2 cooked strips bacon or turkey bacon, crumbled

Rinse the peas in a colander under cold running water until thawed. Drain fully and pat dry with paper towels. In a large bowl, combine the peas, tomatoes, apple, scallions, and dressing and gently toss until well combined. Sprinkle the crumbled bacon over the salad and serve.

Per serving: 124 calories, 6 g protein, 18 g carbohydrates, 4 g total fat, 2 g saturated fat, 11 mg cholesterol, 5 g dietary fiber, 239 mg sodium

Lemon-Horseradish Dressing

Serves 4

3 tablespoons regular or reduced-fat sour cream

1 tablespoon chopped fresh mint

1½ teaspoons lemon juice

1 teaspoon horseradish

Salt and pepper to taste

Whisk together all of the ingredients in a small bowl until well combined.

A WORD ABOUT WELLNESS

Modern science confirms the truth of the "apple a day" adage. Eating apples can contribute to your overall health and is consistently recommended for reduced risks of cardiovascular disease, cancer, asthma, type 2 diabetes, and osteoporosis. Apples have the highest antioxidant activity, after cranberries, of any fruit consumed in the United States, and they are loaded with flavonoids, plant pigments that have anti-inflammatory, anti-allergic, antiviral, and anticancer properties. Apples are also rich in pectin, a soluble fiber that aids in lowering cholesterol and regulating blood sugar.

Grated Carrot Salad

This salad reminds me of Morrison's Cafeteria, a restaurant chain that started in Mobile, Alabama, and later spread throughout the South. It was at Morrison's that I had my first taste of carrot salad. Back then they used mayonnaise for the dressing. This version uses the tartness of lemon and the saltiness of parsley to bring out the sweetness in the carrots. This can quickly be made into a more substantial salad by adding chickpeas. This is a great salad to bring along to a potluck supper.

Serves 4 as a side

1½ pounds carrots, grated

1 cup sliced roasted beets (see page 33), cut into ¼" sticks, or 1 cup slivered red cabbage

1 cup chopped orange sections

¼ cup golden raisins

¼ cup roughly chopped fresh parsley

Bright Lemon Dressing (page 65)

⅓ cup pecans, toasted (see page 30) and chopped

Combine the carrots, beets, orange, raisins, parsley, and dressing in a bowl. Toss, sprinkle with the pecans, and serve.

Per serving: 329 calories, 4 g protein, 35 g carbohydrates, 21 g total fat, 3 g saturated fat, 0 mg cholesterol, 8 g dietary fiber, 223 mg sodium

Red Cabbage, Apple, and Pear Salad with Creamy Maple Dressing

The sweetness of the maple dressing is a nice complement to the tang of the apples and pears in this crunchy coleslaw variation. It makes a wonderful accompaniment to grilled chicken.

Serves 4 as a side

1 Golden Delicious apple, cored and thinly sliced

1 Granny Smith apple, cored and thinly sliced

1 pear, cored and thinly sliced

2 tablespoons lemon juice

½ head red cabbage, shredded

½ small onion, minced

Creamy Maple Dressing

Place the apples, pear, and lemon juice in a large bowl and toss until well coated. Add the cabbage, onion, and dressing and gently toss until well combined.

Per serving: 209 calories, 3 g protein, 32 g carbohydrates, 10 g total fat, 3 g saturated fat, 10 mg cholesterol, 5 g dietary fiber, 36 mg sodium

Creamy Maple Dressing

Serves 4

¼ cup regular or reduced-fat sour cream

2 tablespoons maple syrup

2 tablespoons olive oil

1 tablespoon fresh lemon juice

Whisk together all of the ingredients in a small bowl until well combined. Let stand 15 minutes before using.

Beet Salad
with Yogurt-Dill Dressing

This sweet, tart, colorful salad is wonderful served alongside roasted or grilled meat or chicken.

Serves 4 as a side

1 bunch beets (¾–1 pound), stems trimmed

1 cup low-fat plain yogurt, preferably Greek

¼ cup apple cider vinegar

3 tablespoons honey or maple syrup

1 tart green apple, peeled, cored, and diced

½ cup walnuts or pecans, toasted (see page 30) and chopped

3 scallions (green and white parts), cut into 1" pieces

¼ cup chopped fresh dill

Salt and pepper to taste

Preheat the oven to 400°F. Arrange the beets in a shallow baking dish and cover with aluminum foil. Roast until tender, about 1 hour. (Alternately, simmer the beets in their skins in water to cover until tender, about 40 minutes.) Let cool. Using a paper towel, rub the beets to remove the skins. Dice the beets.

Whisk together the yogurt, vinegar, and honey or maple syrup in a medium bowl until well combined. Add the beets, apple, nuts, scallions, and dill and toss. Season with salt and pepper and serve.

Per serving: 239 calories, 7 g protein, 33 g carbohydrates, 11 g total fat, 2 g saturated fat, 4 mg cholesterol, 4 g dietary fiber, 188 mg sodium

A WORD ABOUT WELLNESS

The beet is a root vegetable that contains powerful antioxidant compounds that help protect against heart disease, birth defects, and certain cancers, especially colon. Both the root and the leaves are edible, although beet greens have more calcium, iron, and the antioxidant potential of vitamins C and A. The root is a very good source of manganese and fiber (in one animal study, beet fiber was found to lower total cholesterol by 30 percent, triglyceride levels by 40 percent, and even increase HDLs). Like bananas, spinach, tomatoes, and asparagus, beets are a good source of potassium, which naturally lowers blood pressure. They are also high in sugar. If you are monitoring your blood sugar levels, take this into consideration.

Marinated Carrot and Red Cabbage Salad

This colorful salad can be made ahead and travels well. It's perfect for picnics and barbecues.

Serves 4 as a side

3 tablespoons white wine vinegar

2 tablespoons vegetable oil

1 tablespoon sesame oil

2½ teaspoons brown sugar

Salt and pepper to taste

3 cups shredded carrots

1½ teaspoons chopped fresh cilantro

Pinch of garlic powder

2 cups shredded red cabbage

Whisk together the vinegar, vegetable oil, sesame oil, sugar, and salt and pepper until well combined. Transfer the marinade to a sealable container. Add the carrots and gently toss until well coated. Cover and refrigerate overnight.

Just before serving, add the cilantro and garlic powder to the carrot mixture and gently toss until well combined. To serve, arrange the shredded red cabbage on a large platter and place the marinated carrots on top.

Per serving: *148 calories, 1 g protein, 13 g carbohydrates, 11 g total fat, 1 g saturated fat, 0 mg cholesterol, 3 g dietary fiber, 140 mg sodium*

A WORD ABOUT WELLNESS

According to the *Journal of the American Medical Association,* foods boasting the antioxidant vitamins C, E, and A can lower your risks of developing dementia and Alzheimer's disease, the devastating neurological condition that affects an increasing number of Americans over age 65. One study followed 3,718 seniors living in the Chicago area for 6 years and reported a significant reduction (about 40 percent) in cognitive decline among people who ate at least 2.8 servings of vegetables and fruits a day compared with those who ate less than 1 serving. Blueberries, broccoli, carrots, spinach, citrus fruits, and nuts and seeds are just some foods with very healthy amounts of these vitamins.

Apple Slaw

This is a sweet and tangy variation of traditional coleslaw. Serve it alongside grilled or roasted pork.

Serves 4 as a side

2 Granny Smith apples, cored and shredded

2 tablespoons lemon juice

1 cup halved red seedless grapes

2 cups shredded red cabbage

3 tablespoons reduced-fat mayonnaise

2 tablespoons vegetable oil

2 teaspoons brown sugar

½ teaspoon ground cinnamon

Toss the apples with the lemon juice in a large bowl. Stir in the grapes and red cabbage. In a small bowl, combine the mayonnaise, oil, sugar, and cinnamon until well mixed. Pour the mixture over the apple mixture and gently toss until well combined.

Per serving: 161 calories, 1 g protein, 23 g carbohydrates, 9 g total fat, 1 g saturated fat, 0 mg cholesterol, 3 g dietary fiber, 110 mg sodium

Potato Salad with Bread and Butter Pickle Dressing

The sweet and sour taste of bread and butter pickles makes this potato salad anything but ordinary on a luncheon buffet table. A mini-food processor makes short work of chopping the pickles and red onion for the dressing.

Serves 4 as a side

1 pound Yukon Gold potatoes

Salt to taste

½ red bell pepper, seeded and diced

½ green bell pepper, seeded and diced

2 ribs celery, chopped

Bread and Butter Pickle Dressing

4 cups bite-size pieces red leaf lettuce

Combine the potatoes and salted water to cover in a saucepan. Bring to a boil, reduce the heat, and simmer until tender when pierced with the tip of a small knife, about 25 minutes. Drain, peel, and cut into 1" cubes.

In a bowl, combine the potatoes, red pepper, green pepper, celery, and dressing and toss. Divide the lettuce among 4 plates. Spoon the salad on top and serve.

Per serving: 146 calories, 5 g protein, 30 g carbohydrates, 1 g total fat, 1 g saturated fat, 2 mg cholesterol, 3 g dietary fiber, 266 mg sodium

Bread and Butter Pickle Dressing

Serves 4

6 tablespoons low-fat plain yogurt, preferably Greek

¼ cup chopped bread and butter pickles

¼ cup buttermilk

2 tablespoons ketchup

2 tablespoons chopped fresh parsley, or 1 teaspoon dried

1 tablespoon chopped red onion

Whisk together all of the ingredients in a small bowl until combined.

Grated Beet and Sweet Potato Salad

Both beets and sweet potatoes can be eaten raw, and are especially nice when grated. Here the raw beets turn the grated sweet potato a lovely pink color.

1 small sweet potato, peeled and grated on the large holes of a grater (2 cups)

2 beets, peeled and grated on the large holes of a grater (about 2 cups)

2 oranges, peeled and chopped, juices reserved

¼ cup white balsamic vinegar

1 tablespoon red wine vinegar

⅓ cup olive oil

¼ cup orange juice

¼ cup chopped fresh parsley, or 1 tablespoon dried

1 teaspoon ground cumin

Salt and pepper to taste

4 cups bite-size pieces red leaf lettuce

Toss together the sweet potato, beets, oranges and their juice, balsamic vinegar, wine vinegar, oil, orange juice, parsley, cumin, and salt and pepper. Let marinate 15 minutes.

Place the lettuce on a serving platter, spoon the salad over, and serve.

Per serving: 260 calories, 2 g protein, 23 g carbohydrates, 18 g total fat, 3 g saturated fat, 0 mg cholesterol, 4 g dietary fiber, 125 mg sodium

Cabbage and Cashew Salad

Cashews are slightly lower in calories than other nuts, and rich in healthy minerals. In this salad they provide a welcome nutty crunch.

Serves 4 as a side

4 cups finely shredded napa cabbage

1 small red onion, diced

½ red bell pepper, seeded and finely chopped

¼ cup white wine vinegar

¼ cup olive oil

1 tablespoon sugar

Pinch cayenne pepper

Salt and pepper to taste

½ cup cashews

Combine the cabbage, onion, and red pepper in a large bowl. In a separate bowl, whisk the vinegar, oil, sugar, cayenne, and salt and pepper until blended. Pour over the salad and gently toss until combined. Let stand for 15 minutes. Sprinkle cashews over the salad just before serving.

Per serving: 256 calories, 4 g protein, 14 g carbohydrates, 22 g total fat, 4 g saturated fat, 0 mg cholesterol, 2 g dietary fiber, 87 mg sodium

Sweet Carrot Salad

Glazed carrots are traditionally made with butter and sugar. For this salad, they're glazed with olive oil and sugar and finished with Parmesan cheese and a bright Lemon-Honey Dressing.

Serves 4 as a side

1 pound carrots, peeled and sliced on an angle ½" thick

1 tablespoon olive oil

1 tablespoon sugar

Salt to taste

½ cup sliced (½") scallions (green and white parts)

½ cup chopped fresh parsley, or 2 tablespoons dried

¼ cup grated Parmesan cheese

4–6 cups bite-size pieces soft lettuce, such as butter or red leaf lettuce

Lemon-Honey Dressing (page 36)

Place the carrots in a large saucepan or deep skillet. Add the olive oil, sugar, and salt to taste. Add water to barely cover the carrots, and bring to a boil. Reduce the heat and simmer, uncovered, until the carrots are tender but still have tooth and all of the water has evaporated, about 15 minutes. Continue cooking, shaking the pan every now and then, until the carrots are lightly browned and glazed, about 5 minutes longer. (If the water evaporates before the carrots are completely cooked, add a little more water.)

Transfer the carrots to a bowl and let cool 10 minutes. Add the scallions, parsley, and Parmesan and toss. Add the greens and dressing, toss again, and serve.

Per serving: 291 calories, 4 g protein, 23 g carbohydrates, 22 g total fat, 4 g saturated fat, 4 mg cholesterol, 5 g dietary fiber, 310 mg sodium

A WORD ABOUT WELLNESS

Carotenoids are fat-soluble red, yellow, and orange pigments found especially in the peels and skins of fruits and vegetables such as tomatoes, sweet potatoes, carrots, and mangoes, to name only some. They are also found in dark green leafy vegetables, but their pigments are blocked by chlorophyll. They are phytochemicals and act as antioxidants in protecting us from cell damage that can cause cancers, cardiovascular disease, and the effects of aging. Lutein, lycopene, and beta-carotene are among the better-known carotenoids.

Chapter 7

Dessert Salads

If you ask most children what their favorite part of the meal is, it doesn't surprise anyone when they all answer, "dessert"! It shouldn't surprise you either that The Salad Man has some favorite dessert salads up his sleeve! The recipes in this section are certain to please children and grown-ups alike. That's a tall order, but our dessert salads meet the challenge as with Banana Pudding Salad (page 205), one of my all-time favorites.

Here are some pointers that you should keep in mind when creating the perfect salad to satisfy every dessert lover:

- Dessert salads can oftentimes double as breakfast salads. Add yogurt, granola, or your favorite cereal to complete the healthy breakfast meal.

- Colors and textures are important. A dessert salad should showcase color and feature at least two different textures, sometimes three—fruit, vegetables, and nuts.

- Though most desserts are somewhat sweet, a dessert salad shouldn't be cloying. Sweetness definitely has to be present, but not necessarily dominant.

- Dessert salads are your signature to end a great meal. Have fun, use color, and celebrate flavor.

Enjoy!

Dessert Salads

*Salad Man Selects recipes

Nectarine Salad with Blue Cheese and Raspberry Vinaigrette

The combination of fruit and cheese in this salad makes for a perfect dessert course. Serve the elegant and colorful dish during the summer when nectarines are in season and at peak flavor.

Serves 4 as a dessert

1 head radicchio, separated into whole leaves

4 ripe nectarines, peeled, pitted, and sliced

1 cup seedless green grapes, each halved

4 ounces blue cheese, crumbled

Raspberry Vinaigrette

¼ cup roughly chopped walnuts

Arrange the radicchio leaves on a large serving platter and top with the nectarine slices. Sprinkle with the grape halves, then the blue cheese. Drizzle the vinaigrette over the salad, sprinkle with the walnuts, and serve.

Per serving: 424 calories, 9 g protein, 31 g carbohydrates, 32 g total fat, 8 g saturated fat, 21 mg cholesterol, 2 g dietary fiber, 472 mg sodium

Raspberry Vinaigrette

Serves 4

⅓ cup vegetable oil

2 tablespoons raspberry vinegar

1 tablespoon raspberry preserves or jam

Salt and pepper to taste

Whisk together all of the ingredients in a small bowl until well combined.

A WORD ABOUT WELLNESS

Apricots, peaches, and nectarines are all good sources of carotenes and flavonoids such as lycopene and lutein (which give them their great yellow-orange colors), as well as vitamins A and C, potassium, iron, and fiber. They are also relatively low in calories. One medium peach or nectarine or three apricots (a 3½ -ounce serving) averages just 49 calories. The beneficial phytochemicals in these fruits help protect you against heart disease, macular degeneration (a disease of the aging eyes), and some cancers. Apricots, and less so peaches, contain beta-cryptoxanthin, a carotenoid that studies demonstrate can reduce lung cancer risk by 30 percent.

Pear and Raspberry Salad with Cheddar Cheese

This salad is so simple, but so very perfect for dessert or a summer brunch. It's like a cheese plate and fruit course all in one!

Serves 4 as a dessert

2 ripe pears

4 red leaf lettuce leaves

8 ounces low-fat plain yogurt, preferably Greek

½ pint raspberries

½ cup grated Cheddar cheese

Halve and core the pears and thinly slice lengthwise. Place a lettuce leaf on each of 4 small plates. Place a spoonful of yogurt on each leaf. Using half a pear per plate, fan the slices and lean against the yogurt. Scatter the raspberries around, sprinkle with the cheese, and serve.

Per serving: 154 calories, 9 g protein, 19 g carbohydrates, 5 g total fat, 3 g saturated fat, 15 mg cholesterol, 5 g dietary fiber, 114 mg sodium

Strawberries and Figs with Balsamic Vinegar

Figs and strawberries, both in season during early to mid-summer, pair beautifully in this simple and elegant dessert salad.

Serves 4 as a dessert

1 pint strawberries, hulled and halved

4 ripe figs, quartered

2 tablespoons balsamic vinegar

1 teaspoon sugar

Toss the strawberries and figs with the vinegar and sugar to combine thoroughly. Divide the fruit among 4 small bowls or stemmed glasses, pour over any remaining vinegar, and serve.

Per serving: 69 calories, 1 g protein, 17 g carbohydrates, 1 g total fat, 0 g saturated fat, 0 mg cholesterol, 2 g dietary fiber, 4 mg sodium

Summer Salad with Maple Syrup

Try any combination of ripe seasonal fruits in this easy salad. The amount of maple syrup to use depends on the sweetness of the fruit.

Serves 4 as a dessert

7–8 cups of any of the following fruits: raspberries, blueberries, strawberries, watermelon, peaches, plums, nectarines, pears, and apples

1–2 tablespoons real maple syrup or honey

¼ cup slivered almonds

Combine the fruit in a large serving bowl and chill.

When ready to serve, gently stir in the maple syrup, starting with 1 tablespoon and adding by the teaspoonful to taste. Sprinkle with the almonds and serve.

Per serving: *172 calories, 4 g protein, 34 g carbohydrates, 4 g total fat, 1 g saturated fat, 0 mg cholesterol, 8 g dietary fiber, 4 mg sodium*

Wiley's Wisdom

Always keep a few brown paper bags handy. If you don't have one, on your next trip to the grocery store, be sure to ask for paper instead of plastic when you check out. Why? That simple little bag could make all the difference between unripe and deliciously ripened fruit. When you purchase fruit that hasn't ripened completely, just put it in the bag, close, and fold the top over to seal. Fruits emit natural gases that, when trapped, accelerate the ripening process. Check it in a day or two. Your fruit will probably have ripened to perfection. It's that simple.

Honeydew and Kiwi Salad with Granola and Yogurt

This salad works with a range of melons and berries. Use whatever looks best in the market. If you don't have granola on hand, raisin bran is a good substitute. Try the salad for breakfast, too!

Serves 4 as a dessert

4 cups cubed honeydew melon (see page 27 on cubing watermelon)

½ pint blueberries

2 kiwifruits, peeled, halved lengthwise, and sliced

2 cups low-fat plain yogurt, preferably Greek

1 cup granola

⅓ cup raisins

Combine the melon, blueberries, and kiwi in a large bowl. Divide among 4 plates and top with yogurt, granola, and raisins.

Per serving: *310 calories, 11 g protein, 60 g carbohydrates, 5 g total fat, 2 g saturated fat, 7 mg cholesterol, 6 g dietary fiber, 130 mg sodium*

A WORD ABOUT WELLNESS

In a study that compared the nutritional values of 27 fruits to determine which were the most nutritious, kiwis were the clear winners, over second-place papaya and third-place co-winners mangoes and oranges. Kiwis had one of the most concentrated levels of vitamin C, containing almost two times the amount of this heart-healthy antioxidant as oranges. They are also loaded with fiber and potassium (in the same study, kiwis, papayas, and apricots beat out oranges and bananas as the best low-sodium, high-potassium foods).

Grilled Fruit Salad with Yogurt-Honey Dressing

If you're used to grilling only chicken, burgers, and steak, you're in for a real treat with this salad. Grilling brings out the sweetness in fruits, and it is an unusual and easy alternative to raw fruit salad. The fruit may be grilled on an outdoor grill, on a grill pan, or under the broiler. The juicier the fruit, the sweeter the taste, because of the caramelization that grilling creates. Fruit grills quickly, so be sure to watch it and turn it often.

Serves 4 as a dessert

1 tablespoon canola oil

1 small pineapple, quartered and cored

4 large nectarines, pitted and halved

2 cups halved strawberries

1 cup blueberries

Yogurt-Honey Dressing

Prepare a medium-hot grill or grill pan or preheat the broiler. Rub the oil all over the pineapple and nectarines. Grill or broil the fruit, turning once, until grill marks appear and the fruit is slightly softened: about 8 minutes for the nectarines and 15 minutes for the pineapple (you won't get grill marks if you broil). Let the fruit cool completely.

When cool, cut the fruit into 1-inch pieces, capturing any juices. Transfer the fruit and its juices to a large bowl. Add the strawberries, blueberries, and dressing. Toss gently and serve immediately.

Per serving: 229 calories, 5 g protein, 47 g carbohydrates, 5 g total fat, 1 g saturated fat, 2 mg cholesterol, 6 g dietary fiber, 24 mg sodium

Yogurt-Honey Dressing

Serves 4

You can make this dressing ahead of time and refrigerate for up to a day.

½ cup low-fat plain yogurt, preferably Greek

1 tablespoon honey

1 teaspoon fresh lemon juice

Whisk all of the ingredients together in a bowl until well combined.

Wiley's Wisdom

There is nothing like the rich and delicious taste of honey in a fresh fruit salad. Not only does it add succulent sweetness, it also causes the fruit to glisten. Use honey sparingly, for it contains more calories measure for measure than table sugar. In fact, honey is primarily all sugar, as it has significant amounts of glucose, fructose, and sucrose.

Molded Peach-Blueberry Salad

This delicious summer salad is served from a pie plate, but you also can make individual desserts in pretty serving dishes for a different presentation.

Serves 4 as a dessert

1 envelope (2¼ teaspoons) powdered unflavored gelatin

3 tablespoons cold water

1½ cups diced ripe peaches (2 medium)

¼ cup sugar

Finely grated zest of 1 lemon

Juice of ½ lemon

¼ teaspoon salt

1 pint blueberries (2¼ cups)

1 cup low-fat plain yogurt, preferably Greek

Sprinkle the gelatin over the water in a small bowl. Set aside for 10 minutes.

Meanwhile, combine the peaches, sugar, lemon zest, lemon juice, and salt in a saucepan. Cook over medium heat, stirring occasionally, until syrupy and only a few pieces of peach remain. Stir in the softened gelatin until melted. Remove the mixture from the heat and stir in the blueberries, then the yogurt. When everything is well combined, transfer to a 9-inch round glass or ceramic pie plate.

Chill in the refrigerator, uncovered, until set, about 2 hours. Cut into wedges and serve.

Per serving: *161 calories, 6 g protein, 34 g carbohydrates, 2 g total fat, 1 g saturated fat, 4 mg cholesterol, 3 g dietary fiber, 193 mg sodium*

A WORD ABOUT WELLNESS

Color may be your simplest clue as to how to choose the most nutritious foods. Look for those fruits and vegetables with the deepest, darkest hues and you will find a mother lode of concentrated vitamins, minerals, and phytochemicals. The more antioxidants in the skin, the darker the color of the food. For example, extremely high levels of the flavonoid anthocyanin give blueberries their deep purple skin, as well as contribute to their extraordinary antioxidant and anti-inflammatory powers. It follows that lighter skinned berries contain lesser amounts of anthocyanin and therefore lesser antioxidant values.

Fruit Salad Boat

This recipe describes a celebratory presentation for any fruit salad, with very little work. If you find an orange-fleshed melon, the colors—orange, green, red, and blue—go particularly well together.

Serves 4 as a dessert

½ cantaloupe or honeydew melon, seeds removed

2 kiwifruits, peeled with a vegetable peeler, quartered, and sliced ½" thick

2 cups halved hulled strawberries

1 pint blueberries (2¼ cups)

¼ cup orange juice

Juice of ½ lemon

¼ cup sliced almonds

To create the "boat," cut balls from the melon half: Place a melon baller, rounded side up, against the flesh of the melon and press down to cut into the flesh (you may see the juices bubble up through the hole in the rounded side of the baller). Swivel the melon baller to cut out a ball of fruit and transfer to a bowl. Continue until most of the melon flesh has been cut into balls. Scrape out the remnants of the melon with a spoon and add that to the bowl (or just eat it).

Add the kiwi, strawberries, blueberries, orange juice, and lemon juice to the melon balls. Cover the salad and boat and refrigerate separately until well chilled, about 2 hours. Stir the salad gently a few times to incorporate the juices.

Transfer the salad with its juices to the melon boat, sprinkle with almonds, and serve.

Per serving: 157 calories, 3 g protein, 32 g carbohydrates, 4 g total fat, 0 g saturated fat, 0 mg cholesterol, 6 g dietary fiber, 15 mg sodium

A WORD ABOUT WELLNESS

With 90 percent water and 227 total calories, a cantaloupe is a weight-loss staple and one of the five most frequently purchased fruits in the United States. This nutrient-rich fruit provides fiber, folic acid, and B vitamins, along with potassium and beta-carotene in abundance. One cup of cubed cantaloupe supplies more than 400 milligrams of potassium; potassium consumption is positively linked with lower rates of blood pressure, heart disease, and stroke. Beta-carotene, which the body converts to vitamin A, helps prevent the formation of plaque along arterial walls.

Ambrosia Salad

If you'd ever had Mrs. Frankie Davis's Ambrosia Salad, you wouldn't soon forget it. Each year we look forward to Christmastime, when we get to sample her delicious recipe, which is similar to the one here. In Greek and Roman mythology, *ambrosia* refers to the food of the gods, with delicious flavor and fragrance. That would make sense, as this salad is absolutely heavenly!

Serves 4 as a dessert or side

One 11-ounce can mandarin oranges, drained

2 bananas, sliced

1 cup drained canned pineapple tidbits

1 cup red or green seedless grapes

1 cup flaked sweetened coconut

1 cup miniature marshmallows

½ cup reduced-fat sour cream

Boston lettuce leaves

Combine the oranges, bananas, pineapple, grapes, coconut, marshmallows, and sour cream in a bowl and stir to mix. Place lettuce leaves on a platter, top with the salad, and serve.

Per serving: 288 calories, 4 g protein, 53 g carbohydrates, 9 g total fat, 7 g saturated fat, 12 mg cholesterol, 5 g dietary fiber, 81 mg sodium

Banana Pudding Salad

Banana pudding was my father's favorite dessert. He sure would have loved this salad version, where fruits and yogurt are pureed to create a rich puddinglike dessert. Many supermarkets now carry Greek yogurt, which is thicker than regular yogurt. Use it for this dish if you can find it. Even the low-fat version is deliciously creamy.

Serves 4 as a dessert

1½ cups low-fat plain yogurt, preferably Greek

2 ripe bananas, sliced

1 mango, peeled and diced (see page 53)

1 cup halved hulled strawberries

¾ cup fresh or canned pineapple chunks

4 teaspoons honey

Fresh mint leaves

Combine the yogurt and bananas in a food processor and process to a puree. Add the mango, strawberries, and pineapple and pulse several times just to roughly chop the fruit. Transfer to a bowl, cover, and refrigerate at least 1 hour.

To serve, divide the pudding among 4 small bowls and drizzle each with about 1 teaspoon honey. Garnish with the mint leaves and serve.

Per serving: 192 calories, 6 g protein, 41 g carbohydrates, 2 g total fat, 1 g saturated fat, 6 mg cholesterol, 4 g dietary fiber, 67 mg sodium

Wiley's Wisdom

I know so many people who suffer from high blood pressure. In fact, according to the American Heart Association, more than 43 million adults over 25 have high blood pressure. This disease can contribute to stroke, heart disease, and heart attack. Potassium is a nutrient that naturally aids in lowering blood pressure, and bananas are a good source of potassium. If you have friends or family members who suffer from or worry about high blood pressure, encourage them to ask their physicians about incorporating more potassium-rich foods like bananas into their diets.

Tropical Rum Punch Salad

The ideal ending to a dinner of grilled meat or fish, this salad offers a refreshing adult treat. Its tropical flavors are inspired by a friend from the island of Nevis.

Serves 4 as a dessert

4 cups bite-size pieces pineapple

2 cups seedless watermelon balls or cubes (see page 27)

Juice of 1 lime

2 tablespoons orange juice

2 tablespoons rum

Combine all ingredients in a bowl. Chill well before serving.

Per serving: 120 calories, 1 g protein, 27 g carbohydrates, 1 g total fat, 0 g saturated fat, 0 mg cholesterol, 3 g dietary fiber, 3 mg sodium

Winter Fruit Salad

This salad combines many of winter's best fruits with the chewy texture of dried cranberries and raisins and the crunch of almonds.

Serves 4 as a dessert

2 ripe bananas, sliced on an angle

4 clementines, peeled and sliced

1 papaya or mango, diced

12 jarred prunes, pitted

1 cup low-fat plain yogurt, preferably Greek

½ cup orange juice

⅛ teaspoon pure vanilla extract

¼ cup raisins

¼ cup dried cranberries

⅓ cup sliced almonds

⅓ cup walnuts or pecans, toasted (see page 30) and chopped

In a large serving bowl, combine the bananas, clementines, papaya or mango, and prunes. Stir together the yogurt, orange juice, and vanilla, and pour over the fruit. Sprinkle the raisins, cranberries, almonds, and walnuts or pecans on top and serve.

Per serving: 402 calories, 9 g protein, 73 g carbohydrates, 12 g total fat, 2 g saturated fat, 4 mg cholesterol, 9 g dietary fiber, 50 mg sodium

Maple-Banana Salad

There is nothing more heavenly than the taste of pecans and bananas, unless it's the taste of pecans, bananas, and maple syrup. Make sure you include lots of raisins in the cup of raisin bran called for below.

1 cup low-fat plain yogurt, preferably Greek

4 teaspoons maple syrup

1 tablespoon water

¼ teaspoon pure vanilla extract

2 ripe bananas, quartered lengthwise and diced

½ cup pecans, toasted (see page 30) and broken into pieces

1 cup raisin bran

Stir together the yogurt, maple syrup, water, and vanilla in a medium bowl. Add the bananas and pecans and stir gently. Divide among 4 glass bowls, sprinkle with the raisin bran, and serve.

Per serving: *261 calories, 7 g protein, 36 g carbohydrates, 12 g total fat, 2 g saturated fat, 4 mg cholesterol, 5 g dietary fiber, 135 mg sodium*

Cranberry-Pecan Salad

This dessert salad makes a wonderful and healthy ending to a big Thanksgiving dinner. Serve it on a bed of greens to help usher in the holidays with red and green color. Canned, whole cranberry sauce makes it a cinch to prepare. If you can't find clementines, use 2 tangerines or oranges instead.

Serves 4 as a dessert or side

1 envelope unflavored gelatin (2¼ teaspoons)

3 tablespoons cold water

1 cup orange juice

One 16-ounce can whole cranberry sauce

Juice of 1 lemon

2 clementines, peeled and sectioned, sections halved

⅓ cup pecans, toasted (see page 30) and chopped

Lettuce (optional)

In a small bowl, sprinkle the gelatin over the water in a bowl and let stand 2 minutes.

Heat the orange juice in a saucepan over medium heat until warm to the touch. Pour over the gelatin and stir to dissolve. Stir in the cranberry sauce, lemon juice, clementines, and pecans. Divide among 4 decorative glass, Pyrex, or ceramic cups, cover, and refrigerate until set, 4 to 6 hours. Serve the salads in the cups or unmold onto a bed of lettuce.

Per serving: 285 calories, 35 g protein, 55 g carbohydrates, 7 g total fat, 1 g saturated fat, 0 mg cholesterol, 3 g dietary fiber, 29 mg sodium

Citrus Salad with Nuts and Dried Fruit Dressing

This light and refreshing dessert salad is the perfect last course to a big meal. Your guests will leave feeling satisfied, but not stuffed.

Serves 4 as a dessert

2 navel oranges, peeled and sliced into ¼" rounds

2 tangerines, clementines, or mandarin oranges, peeled and sliced into ¼" rounds

1 pink grapefruit, peeled and sliced into ¼" rounds

¼ cup sliced almonds or pine nuts, toasted (see page 30)

Dried Fruit Dressing

In a large bowl, combine the oranges, tangerines, grapefruit, nuts, and dressing and gently toss to mix. Cover and refrigerate for 30 minutes before serving.

Per serving: 192 calories, 3 g protein, 42 g carbohydrates, 3 g total fat, 0 g saturated fat, 0 mg cholesterol, 5 g dietary fiber, 70 mg sodium

Dried Fruit Dressing

Serves 4

¼ cup chopped dried apples or dried apricots

¼ cup dried cranberries

¼ cup cranberry juice or orange juice

1 tablespoon honey

In a small bowl, soak the dried apples or apricots and cranberries in the juice until soft, 45 minutes. Add the honey and whisk until blended.

A WORD ABOUT WELLNESS

Dried fruits such as raisins, plums, blueberries, cranberries, apricots, dates, and figs are, of course, fresh fruits that have had their moisture content reduced by drying, typically in the sun. (For example, 1 pound of raisins started out as 4 to 5 pounds of grapes.) Besides increasing the fruit's shelf life (making a ready source when the fruit is not in season), drying appears to preserve and concentrate its health benefits, including antioxidant levels (with the exception of vitamin C, which is greatly reduced). One study of blueberries, the fruit with the highest antioxidant levels, showed that dried blueberries had four times the antioxidants of fresh. A caveat: Because they contain less water than fresh, dried fruits also contain more sugar and calories.

Rhubarb-Orange Salad

Before I knew what rhubarb was, I referred to it as red celery! Rhubarb, in season late spring into early summer, does in fact resemble celery with its long stalks. But unlike celery, it is deep red in color and especially tart. The rhubarb in this dish is cooked with a minimal amount of sugar so that it remains somewhat sour, sweetened mostly by the orange. Feel free to add a bit more sugar if you like. The orange rind loses its bitterness and turns mild tasting as it chills and absorbs the sugar. Add fresh strawberries or blueberries if you like. This salad also makes a good breakfast; just add nuts and yogurt.

Serves 4 as a dessert

1 pound rhubarb, trimmed and cut into
   3" pieces

2 oranges (seeded or use navel oranges),
   washed and sliced (with the peel)

1 cup water

⅓ cup sugar

½ cup favorite dried fruit such as raisins,
   currants, cranberries, or apricots

Combine the rhubarb, oranges, water, and sugar in a saucepan and bring to a boil. Reduce the heat, cover, and simmer very gently until the rhubarb is tender and falls apart, about 15 minutes. Let cool. Transfer to a container, cover, and chill for 2 hours or overnight. Sprinkle the dried fruit on top and serve chilled.

Per serving: 173 calories, 2 g protein, 44 g carbohydrates, 1 g total fat, 0 g saturated fat, 0 mg cholesterol, 4 g dietary fiber, 8 mg sodium

Fruity Trail Mix Salad

This salad travels well and can keep for 2 to 3 days in the refrigerator—a great way for kids to get numerous servings of fruit each day.

Serves 4 as a snack

2 cups red seedless grapes

1 cup dried apricots

¾ cup almonds

¼ cup golden raisins

Combine all of the ingredients in a plastic container with a lid. Cover and refrigerate until ready to serve.

Per serving: *200 calories, 5 g protein, 27 g carbohydrates, 9 g total fat, 1 g saturated fat, 0 mg cholesterol, 3 g dietary fiber, 4 mg sodium*

Appendix

Wiley's Winners—Salad Powerhouses

TOP 15 FRUITS							
	Brain Food	Rich in Fiber	Heart Health	Immunity Booster	Vision Health	Vitamin C Source	Cancer Fighter
Apples		X	X			X	
Apricots	X	X	X	X	X	X	X
Avocados			X				X
Bananas			X			X	
Blueberries	X	X	X	X		X	X
Cantaloupe			X	X	X		X
Cherries	X		X				X
Figs		X	X	X			X
Grapefruits		X	X			X	X
Grapes			X		X		X
Mangoes	X	X				X	X
Oranges			X	X		X	X
Peaches		X		X			X
Strawberries	X		X			X	X
Watermelons		X	X			X	X

TOP 15 VEGETABLES	Brain Food	Rich in Fiber	Heart Health	Immunity Booster	Vision Health	Vitamin C Source	Cancer Fighter
Beets	X		X	X		X	X
Black Beans	X	X	X				X
Broccoli			X		X	X	X
Cabbage		X	X	X		X	X
Carrots		X	X	X	X		X
Cauliflower		X	X			X	X
Chile Peppers			X	X		X	X
Kale	X			X	X	X	X
Mushrooms			X	X			X
Onions			X	X			X
Pea Pods		X				X	
Peppers						X	X
Spinach	X		X	X	X	X	X
Sweet Potatoes		X	X	X	X		X
Tomatoes				X	X	X	X

OTHER INGREDIENTS THAT EMPOWER SALADS	Brain Food	Rich in Fiber	Heart Health	Immunity Booster	Vision Health	Vitamin C Source	Cancer Fighter
Bulgur		X	X				X
Chestnuts			X				X
Garlic			X	X			X
Olive Oil			X				X
Parsley			X	X		X	X
Peanuts		X	X				X
Quinoa		X	X	X	X		X
Walnuts	X		X				

Index

Underscored page references indicate boxed text.

R

Radicchio
about, 13
Radicchio Salad with Chickpeas
and Mango, 148
Radishes
Radish and Fennel Salad, 38
Roasted Spring Vegetable Salad,
131
Raspberries
Pear and Raspberry Salad with
Cheddar Cheese, 196
Tallulah Bankhead Salad, 27
Raspberry jam
Raspberry-Pomegranate
Vinaigrette, 34
Raspberry Vinaigrette, 195
Restaurant salads, ordering, 15–16
Rhubarb
Rhubarb-Orange Salad, 212
Rice
Brown Rice Salad with Feta
Cheese, 179
Brown Rice Seafood Salad,
54–55
Chicken and Wild Rice Salad
with Butternut Squash and
Dried Cherries, 86
Curried Chicken Salad with
Mushrooms and Brown Rice,
74
Kale and Brown Rice Salad, 164
Mexican Brown Rice Salad, 147
New Orleans Dirty Rice Salad, 99
Salmon and Brown Rice Salad,
62–63
Stuffed Bell Pepper Salad,
136–37
Turkey and Wild Rice Salad, 97
Warm Wild Rice Salad with
Swiss Chard, Broccoli, and
Corn, 154
Rosemary, health benefits from,
107

S

Salad bars, choosing items from,
15

Salad bowls, 14–15
Salad dressings. *See* Dressings;
Vinaigrettes
Salad Man Selects
Ambrosia Salad, 204
BLT Salad, 121
Chicken Pasta Salad with
Tomatoes, Spinach, and
Broccoli, 84
Chow-Chow Salad, 172
Fried Green Tomato Salad, 22
Garden Pasta Salad, 171
Green Bean, Corn, and Tomato
Salad, 173
Molded Peach-Blueberry Salad,
202
New Orleans Dirty Rice Salad,
99
Oven-Fried Chicken Salad, 73
Pear and Raspberry Salad with
Cheddar Cheese, 196
"Poke Salet" with Bacon and
Eggs, 127
Pool Room Slaw, 180
Roll Tide Tailgate Salad, 114–15
Southern Potato Salad, 178
Steak and Tomato Salad with
Horseradish Dressing,
110–11
Stuffed Bell Pepper Salad,
136–37
Succotash Salad with Citrus
Vinaigrette, 170
Sweet Potato Pie Salad, 152
Tallulah Bankhead Salad, 27
Tuna-Stuffed Tomatoes, 66
Warm Catfish Salad with
Collards and Watermelon,
64–65
Salads
at restaurants, 15–16
from salad bars, 15
health benefits, 1–2
pantry items for, 9
preparing, equipment for, 14–15
preparing, tips for, 11
salad greens for, 11–13
Salad spinners, 14
Salmon
Salmon and Brown Rice Salad,
62–63

Salmon Salad with Cherry
Tomatoes and Lemon, 61
Squash Salad with Salmon
Teriyaki, 60
Salsa
Fresh Tomato Salsa, 105
Salt, daily intake of, 55
Sauerkraut
Pork and Sauerkraut Salad, 120
Sausages
Mexican Cornbread Salad with
Chicken Sausage, 80
Scallops
Brown Rice Seafood Salad,
54–55
Marinated Vegetable Salad with
Scallops, 57
Scallop Ceviche Salad, 56
Seafood. *See* Fish; Shellfish
Seeds
health benefits, 4, 141
sesame, toasting, 130
Sesame oil
about, 39
Honey-Sesame Dressing, 77
Sesame Dressing, 130, 162
Sesame seeds, toasting, 130
Shallots
Shallot–Red Wine Vinaigrette,
137
Shallot Vinaigrette, 23
Shellfish. *See also* Shrimp
Brown Rice Seafood Salad,
54–55
Marinated Vegetable Salad with
Scallops, 57
Mussel and New Potato Salad,
58–59
mussels, preparing for cooking,
59
Scallop Ceviche Salad, 56
Shrimp
Brown Rice Seafood Salad,
54–55
Cobb Shrimp Salad, 44–45
Greek Salad with Shrimp, 47
grilling, 45
poaching, 45
sautéing, 45
Shrimp and Barley Salad, 50
Shrimp and Pinto Bean Salad, 51

Conversion Chart

These equivalents have been slightly rounded to make measuring easier.

Volume Measurements

U.S.	Imperial	Metric
¼ tsp	–	1 ml
½ tsp	–	2 ml
1 tsp	–	5 ml
1 Tbsp	–	15 ml
2 Tbsp (1 oz)	1 fl oz	30 ml
¼ cup (2 oz)	2 fl oz	60 ml
⅓ cup (3 oz)	3 fl oz	80 ml
½ cup (4 oz)	4 fl oz	120 ml
⅔ cup (5 oz)	5 fl oz	160 ml
¾ cup (6 oz)	6 fl oz	180 ml
1 cup (8 oz)	8 fl oz	240 ml

Weight Measurements

U.S.	Metric
1 oz	30 g
2 oz	60 g
4 oz (¼ lb)	115 g
5 oz (⅓ lb)	145 g
6 oz	170 g
7 oz	200 g
8 oz (½ lb)	230 g
10 oz	285 g
12 oz (¾ lb)	340 g
14 oz	400 g
16 oz (1 lb)	455 g
2.2 lb	1 kg

Length Measurements

U.S.	Metric
¼"	0.6 cm
½"	1.25 cm
1"	2.5 cm
2"	5 cm
4"	11 cm
6"	15 cm
8"	20 cm
10"	25 cm
12" (1')	30 cm

Pan Sizes

U.S.	Metric
8" cake pan	20 × 4 cm sandwich or cake tin
9" cake pan	23 × 3.5 cm sandwich or cake tin
11" × 7" baking pan	28 × 18 cm baking tin
13" × 9" baking pan	32.5 × 23 cm baking tin
15" × 10" baking pan	38 × 25.5 cm baking tin (Swiss roll tin)
1½ qt baking dish	1.5 liter baking dish
2 qt baking dish	2 liter baking dish
2 qt rectangular baking dish	30 × 19 cm baking dish
9" pie plate	22 × 4 or 23 × 4 cm pie plate
7" or 8" springform pan	18 or 20 cm springform or loose-bottom cake tin
9" × 5" loaf pan	23 × 13 cm or 2 lb narrow loaf tin or pâté tin

Temperatures

Fahrenheit	Centigrade	Gas
140°	60°	–
160°	70°	–
180°	80°	–
225°	105°	¼
250°	120°	½
275°	135°	1
300°	150°	2
325°	160°	3
350°	180°	4
375°	190°	5
400°	200°	6
425°	220°	7
450°	230°	8
475°	245°	9
500°	260°	–